SUNRISE AT CORBYN'S COVE, SOUTH ANDAMAN / R. IAN LLOYD

This book is dedicated to the memory of our longtime colleague Jane H. Buxton, who planned this island odyssey with the same style and dedication that she brought to all the books she edited for the Book Division. Her vision guided us in its creation.

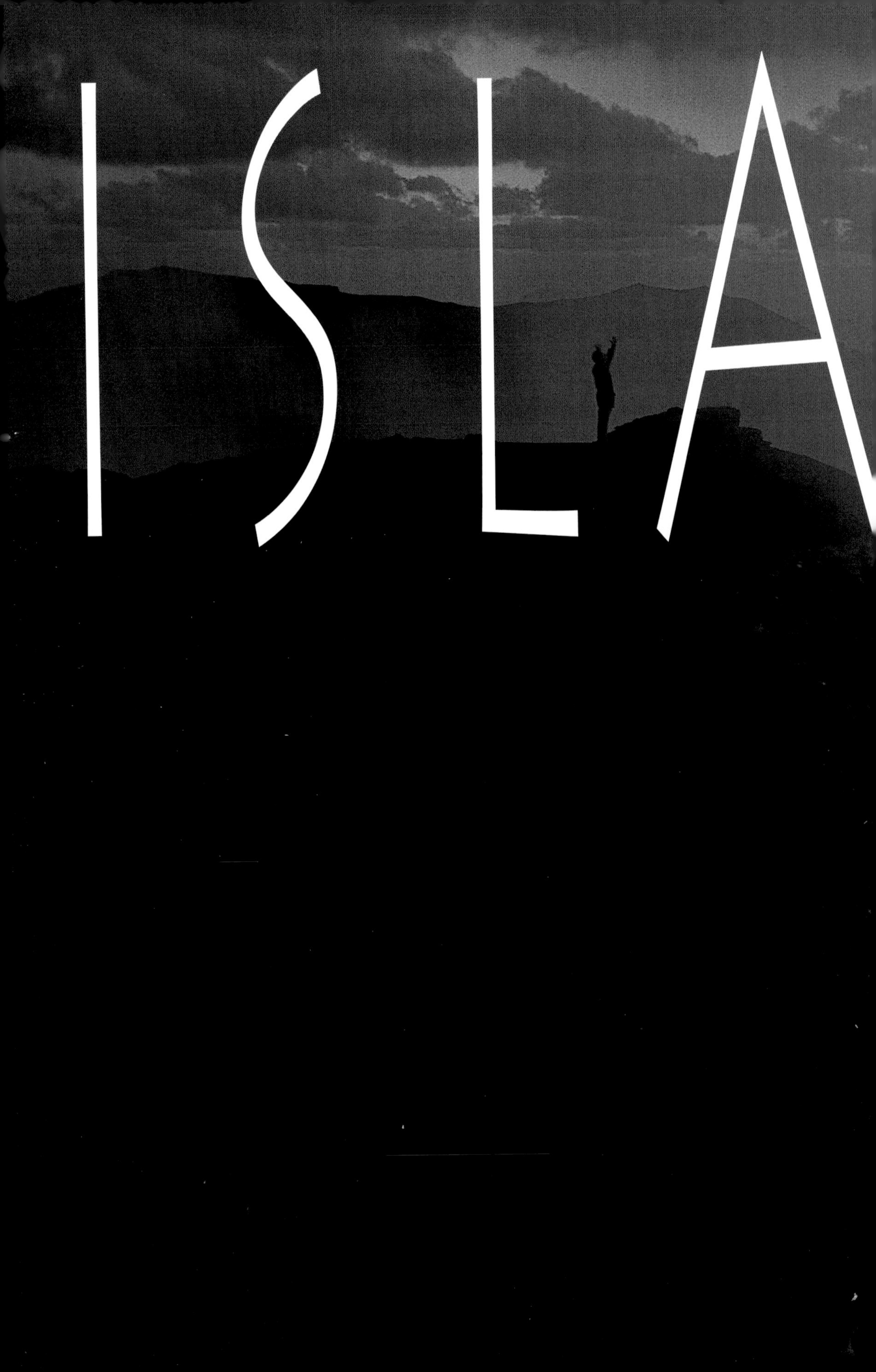
ISLA

NDs

LOST IN TIME

Prepared by the Book Division
National Geographic Society, Washington, D.C.

ABOVE: VIEW OVER CUMBERLAND BAY ON RÓBINSON CRUSOE, JUAN FERNÁNDEZ / MIGUEL LUIS FAIRBANKS

Published by
The National Geographic Society

Reg Murphy
President and Chief Executive Officer

Gilbert M. Grosvenor
Chairman of the Board

Nina D. Hoffman
Senior Vice President

Prepared by
The Book Division

William R. Gray
Vice President and Director

Charles Kogod
Assistant Director

Barbara A. Payne
*Editorial Director and
Managing Editor*

Staff for this book

Jane H. Buxton
Project Editor

John G. Agnone
Illustrations Editor

Mary B. Dickinson
Text Editor

Marianne R. Koszorus
Art Director

Elisabeth B. Booz
Catherine C. Fox
Victoria Garrett Jones
Anne E. Withers
Researchers

Martha C. Christian
Consulting Editor

Carl Mehler
Map Editor

Peter A. Jolicoeur
Map Research

Michelle H. Picard
Map Production

Richard S. Wain
Production Project Manager

Jennifer L. Burke
Illustrations Assistant

Dale-Marie Herring
Peggy J. Purdy
Staff Assistants

*Manufacturing and
Quality Management*

George V. White
Director

John T. Dunn
Associate Director

Vincent P. Ryan
Manager

Polly P. Tompkins
Executive Assistant

Elisabeth MacRae-Bobynskyj
Indexer

CONTENTS

ISLANDS
LOST IN TIME

Introduction

By Leslie Allen

magined or real, islands have always had a special way of evoking lost or elusive worlds. The ancient Greeks located paradise itself on the Isles of the Blest. And they recalled the legendary island of Atlantis—said by Plato to have been submerged by an earthquake—so hauntingly that archaeologists today still search for it. From *Treasure Island* to *Peter Pan,* some of childhood's most beloved tales unfold on islands; Daniel Defoe's novel *Robinson Crusoe* was inspired by the real-life adventures of a castaway on the Juan Fernández Islands off the coast of Chile.

"The island wilderness," Mark Twain said, "is the very home of romance and dreams and mystery." But a world girdled by instant communication and diced into minute grids by satellite mapping technology seems an unlikely place to imagine islands lost in time. Mass tourism and development have fundamentally altered many small islands; alien plant and animal species have disrupted fragile ecosystems.

But the reality is surprising: It is an unexpected irony of our shrinking world that some less economically dynamic places are now more isolated than when the world seemed bigger. Here and there remain a few islands where, in different ways, today is still yesterday.

Casting a wide net, this volume takes readers to an eclectic selection of these islands: the Andamans, Pitcairn and Norfolk, Gotland, the Juan Fernández group, and the Aeolians. Others mentioned in this introduction might have been included, had space allowed.

All in all, these islands are diverse. Some are famous, others obscure. Some seem as remote as dimly flickering stars in a night sky, and almost as inaccessible; the words "isle" and "isolated" are, after all, twins that spring from the same Latin root. But a few rise into full view from the mainland, and have had a string of conquerors to show for their accessibility.

Just off the north coast of Sicily, the rockbound Aeolian archipelago bears witness to more than 6,000 years of cultural succession. Ancient, sunburned villages and archaeological treasures bring alive the dense layerings of civilization here—Bronze Age, Greek, Carthaginian, Roman, Norman, among others—that flourished and then withered. Wrapped in wind-whipped sea foam, the islands' stark beauty and fiery volcanoes have also inspired some of the myths and epic poetry that anchor Western civilization to its Mediterranean roots.

Like peaks that snag passing clouds to bring down rain, such islands have caught and kept the richness of the various cultures that have drifted their way over the centuries. The past lasts longer on these islands. But timelessness doesn't mean frozen in time. Not just

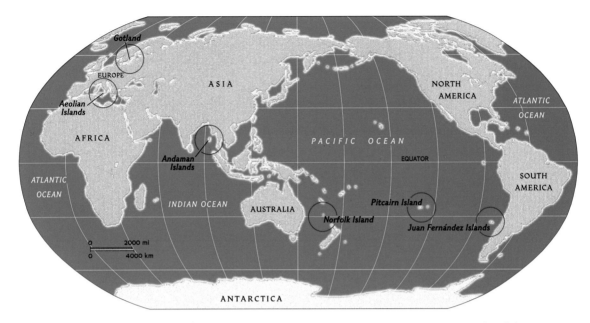

Time takes on a different dimension in island refuges that range across the globe.

museums, these little seagirt worlds retain their character as the winds of time blow through them.

Far to the north, the people of another timeless island, Sweden's Gotland, have earned a modest living from fishing, farming, and quite recently, tourism, since Gotland plummeted from the peak of its golden age in the 14th century. Now almost completely unknown beyond Scandinavia, the island controlled northern European trade for centuries during Roman, Viking, and finally, Hanseatic times. Plague, plunder, and panic ended Gotland's greatness, but spared enough of its fine old buildings that Visby, with its surrounding wall, takes pride of place as the best-preserved medieval city in northern Europe. But even on Gotland,

the past is not entirely an unchanging, well-documented affair. More of it is literally unearthed from time to time, as Gotlanders stumble upon treasure hoards buried in the Viking era more than a thousand years ago.

Westering at least as far as the island of Newfoundland, the Vikings sprinkled island communities across the North Atlantic—and then abandoned most of them. Only many centuries later did European explorers lay lasting claim to the far-flung little islands they found. The rising tide of empire washed over the Indies—East and West—the South Pacific, and a scattering of islands elsewhere. Geopolitical and commercial jockeying played a role in the colonization of even the most remote specks of terra firma.

It is hard to imagine islands more remote than a trio of minute British outposts in the South Atlantic—

St. Helena, Tristan da Cunha, and Ascension. Each lies more than a thousand miles from the mainland, and nearly as far from its nearest island neighbor. None of the islands has commercial air service.

Misfortune washed most of their early visitors ashore. A 16th-century Portuguese nobleman, his face horribly mutilated as a punishment for desertion, hid from the world for years on St. Helena. A 17th-century mariner, marooned on the island as punishment, disinterred a comrade's coffin and frantically paddled it out to sea in pursuit of his ship. (His astounded shipmates, who at first thought a ghost was approaching, finally took pity on the sailor and hauled him aboard.) Augustus Earle, an English artist and traveler who found himself stranded on Tristan in the 1820s, described the sea's deafening roar, the wind rushing down 900-foot volcanic crags, and the mournful screams of nocturnal birds. "No spot in the world can be more desolate," wrote Earle.

The historical event that put the islands on the world map, so to speak, stemmed not only from their remoteness but also from official fears that they might not prove quite isolated enough. In October 1815, HMS *Northumberland* arrived in St. Helena bearing the defeated Napoleon to his final island exile at Longwood Estate, now St. Helena's one tourist draw. Thousands of British soldiers were shipped over to guard the emperor. But that was not enough to calm British nerves: The Royal Navy also took over Ascension and Tristan, establishing garrisons to avert any possible attempt by the French to rescue their famous prisoner.

What are the islands like now? Ascension, a rumbling volcano, has made interesting transitions—from a mid-ocean mailbox for passing 16th-century ships to one of the great cable stations of the British Empire; and finally, to a nerve center of a new kind, a military communications outpost bristling with radar domes, satellite monitors, and computer equipment.

Tristan da Cunha, another volcano, erupted in 1961, forcing the evacuation of its 264 residents to England. All but five returned to the empire's smallest and most remote dependency, there to carry on their quiet lives in an economy made prosperous by the export of rock lobsters. Since their return, many islanders have replaced their thatched roofs with shingled ones less likely to ignite when volcanic cinders rain down upon them. Little else has changed. The *Tristan Times,* published from time to time, carries messages from Buckingham Palace and the colonial administrator, news of the "houtside warld," local announcements, and—in 1996—word that eight ship visits were planned.

The ebb tide of the British Empire finds charming St. Helena high, dry, and curiously lost in time. The island's last industry collapsed in 1966 when the British postal system switched from St. Helena flax to nylon for string to tie up its mail bundles. Unemployment rose, and aid from London fell off. But emigration to the United Kingdom is barred under the British Nationality Act. Many Saints, as they call themselves, now find work on the high seas or in the high-tech world of Ascension, leaving behind St. Helena's gaily painted Regency homes and the whitewashed castle bearing the coat of arms of the Honourable East India Company.

India-bound steamers stopped using St. Helena as a coaling station after the Suez Canal opened in 1869. Then oil made coal obsolete. After the air age dawned, sailings between London and Cape Town—with a stop at St. Helena—became ever scarcer. As improvements in transportation and communication have made the world smaller, St. Helena, paradoxically, has become more remote than ever.

Remoteness, of course, was exactly what some of history's most famous mutineers were seeking when they sailed for Pitcairn, now Britain's last Pacific Ocean colony, in 1789. Finding the island, though, was quite another matter for Fletcher Christian and his companions on the *Bounty,* once they had dispatched Capt. William Bligh and 18 sailors to their fate in an open cutter.

Christian had learned the location of Pitcairn from a chart in Bligh's cabin, but the discoverer, Capt. Philip Carteret, had plotted the island's location some 200 miles off course. In the end, Carteret's error worked to the mutineers' advantage: Sequestered on an island far from its supposed location, they disappeared from the world. On the other hand, their mates who had preferred to be dropped off in Tahiti were discovered and tried in London; three were hanged.

Remote islands have always been inviting hideaways for pirates, mutineers, and others on the wrong side of the law. In 1827, Capt. John Clunies-Ross brought a group that included his wife, family, friends, and some of his ship's crew to settle on the Cocos, or Keeling, Islands in the middle of the Indian Ocean.

Alexander Hare, formerly the governor of a British settlement in Borneo, was already there. Hare had good reason to seek a remote island hideaway: He had acquired a harem of 40 Malay women.

To stave off the sailors' advances to the women, Hare removed his harem to a nearby atoll and tried to placate the men with gifts of rum and roast pig. But the sailors simply waded across the shallow channel to Hare's atoll; eventually all the women deserted their master, who died in Indonesia attempting to gather a new harem.

Island societies frequently create an unexpected mix of groups or factions. In 1856, Nathan Thompson, a rigger from an American whaling ship, landed on Lord Howe Island, some 370 miles off the east coast of Australia. Discovered by the British in 1788, it was named for the First Lord of the Admiralty and already boasted a handful of British settlers.

Thompson arrived with two native women from the Gilbert Islands. He married the older woman; after her death, he married the younger, held by tradition to be a princess. By the 1920s, the island's little society was divided into two fairly distinct factions. The whaler's descendants, all Seventh-day Adventists, observed a Saturday Sabbath; the Church of England's adherents rested and worshiped on Sunday. The Americans decorated their homes with pictures of American heroes such as General Grant and treasured "real American recipes" like pumpkin pie. The British contingent guarded their traditions just as carefully. But all of the islanders joined hands in a thriving communal economy based on the export of palm seeds, the collective ownership of land, and a shared bank account in Sydney.

These days, it is not easy for eccentrics and misfits to find their own remote island retreats, as Smiley Ratliff of Frog Level, Virginia, discovered in 1983. Having made a fortune running coal mines, Ratliff decided he wanted to get as far away as possible from civilization's ills—among which he included Communism, psychology, Big Government, and Elvis Presley. Ratliff needed an uninhabited island, and after circling the globe, finally pinpointed his private Eden on Henderson Island, one of the Pitcairn group.

Price, he told the British Foreign Office, was no object; and Ratliff's promise to start ferry service to Pitcairn and build an airstrip on Henderson helped to prod the unusual negotiations along. But in the end, the cliffbound coral islet turned out to be too much of a real Eden—an untouched trove of native flowering plants, land and sea birds, reef creatures, and protected endemic species—and ecological concerns doomed the deal, to the disappointment of Pitcairn's dwindling community, which was eager for better links to the outside world.

Remote island worlds, isolated for eons, are fragile, vulnerable places, where both natural and human communities hang in the balance. Air links can be a mixed blessing for those islands. A Cessna flies a doctor in for a medical emergency; cargo planes deliver much-needed supplies; tourists fortify the island's economy. Lord Howe Island, now a couple of hours' hop from Sydney, welcomes small numbers of tourists but remains undeveloped; the island, with its rich flora and fauna, is preserved as a world heritage site. The Juan Fernández Islanders have solicited tourism by renaming two of their islands after Robinson Crusoe and Alexander Selkirk—the sailor whose tale inspired Defoe. But the islands so far maintain a small, stable, tradition-bound population even as tourism grows.

On many once-remote islands, though, the balance has been tipped; the outside world has swamped them. Still others are fighting hard for their ancient traditions and their integrity. It is hard to imagine a place with more at stake than India's Andamans, a string of more than 200 small islands in the Bay of Bengal. Most of the archipelago is a wilderness of rain forest and reef that harbors a myriad of land and sea creatures. Only a few of the islands are inhabited; dozens are set aside as national parks, wildlife refuges, and nature reserves.

As a new millennium approaches, Andaman island reserves still shelter one of the world's last hunter-gatherer tribes, the Sentinelese. Another group, the Jarawa, answer the increasingly common trespasses onto their land with fusillades of arrows and spears. A third tribe, the original Andamanese, have been practically wiped out by diseases brought in by outsiders; while a fourth, the Onges, support themselves by working on a fruit plantation as well as by traditional hunting and gathering.

The Indian government has declared the Andamans' tribal reserves off-limits to visitors. But with increasing numbers of land-starved Indians from the densely populated mainland migrating to the Andamans, it becomes ever more difficult to keep the realities of the modern world at bay.

In the Andamans, an imaginary drawbridge that has always been lifted is now falling. Whatever the words "lost in time" may mean in other island worlds, in the Andamans they have become a plea for survival.

THE ANDA

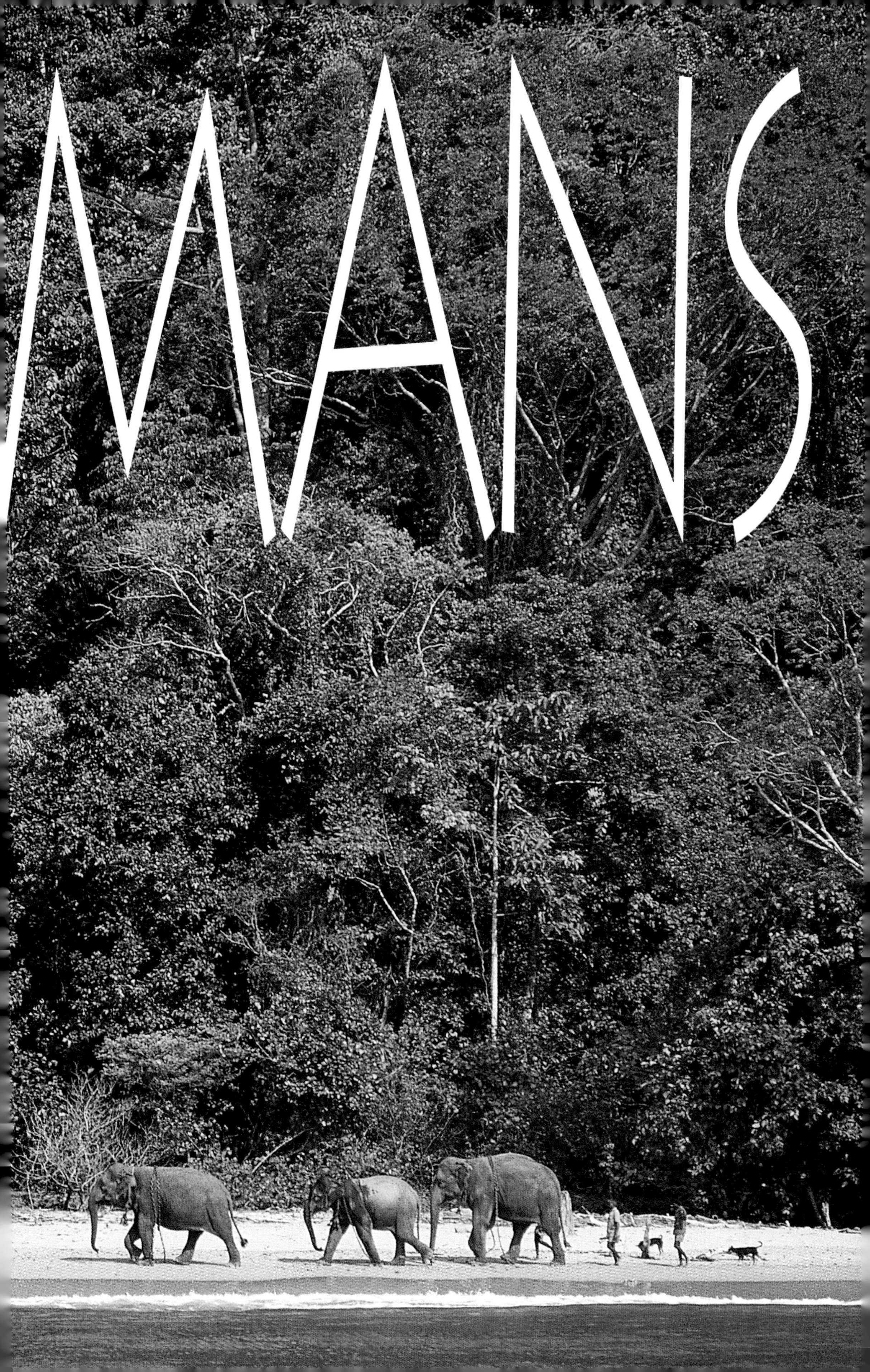
MANS

The Andamans

By Joseph R. Yogerst

Photographs by R. Ian Lloyd

SET IN THE BAY OF BENGAL SOME 800 MILES
FROM THE INDIAN COAST, THE ANDAMAN ISLANDS ARE
THE MOST SECLUDED PART OF INDIA, A PLACE WHERE
ABORIGINAL TRIBES STILL LIVE IN PROTECTED AREAS. A
NOTORIOUS PENAL COLONY IN YEARS PAST, THE ISLANDS
ARE NOW A MELTING POT OF THE MYRIAD ETHNIC AND
RELIGIOUS GROUPS THAT MAKE UP MODERN INDIA.

A fishing boat heads home at sunrise in Corbyn's Cove on South Andaman.
Preceding pages: Elephants pace a training camp for the timber industry at Madhuban.

Krishna devotees at the annual Krishna chanting festival in Govindpur on Middle Andaman rotate duties during 72 consecutive hours of music, dance, and prayer. The event is celebrated after the Hindu festival of Holi.

Following pages: Indian tourists explore Port Blair's notorious Cellular Jail. Completed in 1906, it confined hardened criminals and political prisoners from the mainland in 698 cells. The prison is now maintained as a national memorial to Indians who fought for independence from Britain.

've never taken much stock in ghost stories and other spectral sightings. But if there's one place that sends a chill up my spine, an eerie feeling that someone or something is watching from the shadows, it's Ross Island in India's Andaman Islands.

Much of this foreboding derives from the fact that most of the old colonial settlement is now smothered by jungle. As I explored the ruins it was often difficult to separate buildings from trees. Thick branches were wrapped around the walls of the Presbyterian church. Roots had run amok across the balcony of the chief commissioner's house, and the cemetery was as much a resting-place for fallen coconuts as for residents who never left the island.

This feeling of trepidation also stems from Ross's peculiar history. Founded in 1858 by enterprising Englishmen, the settlement prospered for nearly a hundred years as the capital of the Andaman Islands, one of the far-flung patches of a British Empire that once covered much of the Indian Ocean. As in many imperial outposts, the inhabitants did their best to replicate life back home: weddings and baptisms in quaint English churches, high tea and tennis on sweeping lawns, and Viennese waltzes in the ballroom.

Yet lurking behind this cheerful facade was something sinister: The administrative functions of the dreaded Andaman penal colony that embraced both political prisoners and brutal killers—an island exile from which few inmates ever returned home.

Not far from Ross are other relics of that malevolent era: Viper Island with its wooden gallows, and the Cellular Jail in Port Blair, once one of the most infamous prisons in the British Empire. Yet without this notorious history—and the fact that colonial authorities kept the islands untamed and largely unsettled to deter escapes—the Andamans wouldn't be what they are today: One of the last great wilderness areas of south Asia, a land of strange animals, aboriginal tribes, and a turquoise coast largely untouched by late 20th-century life.

There are more than 200 islands in the chain, and although they are governed by New Delhi, the Andamans are actually closer to Myanmar (Burma) and Sumatra than to any point on the Indian mainland. Most of the 400,000 inhabitants live on the three largest islands—North, South, and Middle Andaman—which means the majority of the islands are still uninhabited and undeveloped. More than 80 percent of the land is covered in tropical forest. Along the coast are thriving mangrove swamps, the habitat of a wide array of creatures from tiny mudskippers to enormous saltwater crocodiles and dugongs that dwell in tidal creeks. There are hundreds of miles of pristine coral reef. And the beaches are almost postcard perfect, with a backdrop of coconut palms and fine, white sand that seems to melt beneath your feet.

Arriving in early spring, before monsoon rains and cyclones sweep through the Bay of Bengal, photographer Ian Lloyd and I wanted to traverse the Andaman Islands from south to north, starting at Port Blair and finishing in Diglipur—a journey of two hundred miles to the north that would take us into every major ecosystem and through all of the primary towns. Our initial idea was to drive the entire length of the Andaman Trunk Road (ATR), a grand name for a modest two-lane highway with several ferry crossings. But after arrival in Port Blair, it became readily apparent that things would not go as planned. There were events beyond our control—beyond the control of the Indian government—such as an indigenous tribe called the Jarawa.

THE JARAWA ARE ONE OF four hunter-gatherer groups that inhabit the Andamans. They are short of stature, with extremely dark skin. For many years they were thought to be a "lost" African tribe that had somehow strayed into the Bay of Bengal, until anthropolgists ascertained their kinship to other Negrito peoples of the Asia-Pacific region.

Given their dwindling numbers—none of the tribes boasts more than a few hundred inhabitants and one group (the Great Andamanese) is down to less than 40—and their general hostility toward outsiders, the Indian government decided long ago to protect them within the confines of reservations that are off-limits to all outsiders. For most of this century, the delicate balance between tribal life and modern Andaman civilization has endured. But in recent years, settlers from mainland India have begun encroaching on tribal land.

Responding to this invasion the only way they knew how, the Jarawa began ambushing vehicles and attacking villages along the ATR. Authorities told us that several settlers had been killed by Jarawa arrows during the past year, and shortly after our arrival the road was closed after renewed Jarawa attacks.

"Our relationship with these tribes is on very shaky ground," said Anstice Justin, a Nicobar Islander who heads the Andaman office of the Anthropological Survey of India. "There have been several incidents of Jarawa attacking settlement areas, but there is strong evidence that they were provoked...that settlers are interfering in tribal areas."

The gruesome nature of the deaths—the bodies were mutilated and left in the forest as a warning to other would-be trespassers—had provoked an emotional response in nearby farming communities including rumors of cannibalism. "We have no proof of that," said Justin. "The Jarawa have always mutilated the bodies of their enemies. Some people think it's their way to prevent evil spirits from leaving the body."

"We're here to ensure the best way of survival of these people," Justin told us. "Our suggestion is to proceed at a slow pace so as not to harm their indigenous culture. But some people in the government feel it should be speeded up as part of national integration." As a result, the Andaman government has recently stepped up "contact missions" to the most isolated groups—the Jarawa and Sentinelese—in an effort to quell their hostility and acclimatize them to outsiders. Justin was fundamentally opposed to increased contact, but admitted that the expeditions gave him a rare opportunity to study tribal culture.

The latest contact mission was leaving that night on a week-long journey to North Sentinel Island and the western shores of South and Middle

Tree roots and vines engulf a house on Ross Island, the former seat of British colonial rule in the Andamans. The uninhabited ruins have been reclaimed by jungle.

Andaman where the Jarawa reside. We begged Justin for a place on the boat, but he reminded us that no foreigners had ever been granted permission to travel into tribal areas. He promised us a full debriefing on his return.

Next morning, Ian and I began our quest for an alternative means by which to explore the Andamans. The trail eventually led to Shanthi Shipping, a small company that handles about a dozen interisland vessels. The manager wasn't sure if any boats were available— most were busy shipping timber and other local commodities—but he would assess the situation and get back to us.

Meanwhile, we set about exploring Port Blair and environs. The Andaman capital is really more a cluster of villages than a true city, a low-rise skyline that ambles across several hills, with none of

the buildings much taller than a coconut tree. In stark contrast to mainland India, Port Blair exudes a laid-back attitude that slows everything to a snail's pace. No one rushes about—not even the taxi drivers in their vintage Ambassadors— tardiness is accepted as a normal part of life, and stress is virtually absent.

Port Blair, like all of the Andaman communities, also exhibits an amazing tolerance, forming a melting pot that isn't boiling over with racial and religious tension. Hindus, Muslims, Christians, Sikhs, and others live side by side, respectful of one another's beliefs and traditions, turning their back on the internecine rivalries that plague much of mainland India. "In India we have a unique social system—different castes and different religions," says Mitra Kaushik, a history teacher at Nehru College in Port Blair. "But in Andaman we don't have these things. People are much more tolerant here. So in a sense, the British transportation and penal policy accomplished what all the politicians have been trying to do for fifty years on the mainland."

DURING THE NEXT WEEK, as we waited for word from Shanthi Shipping, I got to know many of the neighborhoods in Port Blair. I walked the back streets and dark lanes of Aberdeen Bazaar, a thriving market quarter where you can buy everything from silk saris and Darjeeling tea to Hindi pop star posters. I sat outside the harbormaster's office and eyed the action in Phoenix Bay, a constant ebb and flow of ferries, fishing boats, steamers, and sleek gray cutters of the Indian Navy.

In Haddo, I attended Mass at the Catholic cathedral and then tried my luck at cricket with local boys who had organized a Sunday afternoon pick-up game in a vacant lot. On Marine Hill, with its sweeping views of the harbor, I watched dhobi wallahs beat their washing against stones in a ritual that hasn't changed in a thousand years. And in Dugnabad, an old residential district that hugs the wall of the Cellular Jail, I mingled with the "local born"—descendants of pre-1942 convicts—men such as Gauri Shanker Pandey, who proudly traces his roots through several generations of political prisoners.

Over tea and biscuits in his living room, Pandey revealed his family history: "My great-grandfather became entangled in politics and was sent to Andaman in the 1870s. The rule was that a convict who had good character for a certain period would be allowed to leave the prison and settle down here. And if he was in a position to support a family, he was allowed to marry a woman from the convict population." Thus the prison became a prime

vehicle for colonizing these islands.

Shanthi Shipping made good the following day on their promise of finding us a boat. And that news prompted a giant sigh of relief: We were finally on our way north. At seven the next morning we were ready to cast off from Phoenix Bay. Our boat—a motor launch, the ML *Tanveer*—was less than impressive at first glance, a Thai fishing boat confiscated by the Indian Navy, sold at auction, and then converted to passenger use. But it was all we had.

None of the seven crew members had ever been north of Port Blair, so the voyage was an adventure for them also. But our captain had enough experience for everyone aboard. His name was Christopher Forbes, a tall man with broad shoulders, blue eyes, and curly black hair—an Anglo-Indian from Bombay with more than a quarter century of sailing under his belt. Forbes had prepared a special ceremony on the dock, a combination bon voyage and good luck ritual. One of the crewmen dabbed our faces with colored powder and slipped hibiscus blooms behind our ears. Our good fortune assured, it was time to depart.

We cleared the mouth of Port Blair and chugged slowly into the open waters of the Andaman Sea. Flying fish skimmed across the waves in front of the bow, and in the distance I could see a couple of fishing boats with lateen sails, but otherwise the sea lanes were vacant. The upper reaches of South Andaman consisted of coconut groves and jungle-covered mountains.

Farther up the coast I spotted something so incongruous that I thought it must surely be a mirage: half a dozen

elephants lumbering through the surf. I blinked and they disappeared into a coconut grove beside the beach. But Forbes assured me that it wasn't my imagination. It was our first landfall, an isolated village called Madhuban, which plays host to the most famous school in the Andamans—an educational institute for elephants.

Adult elephants selected to work in the Andaman timber industry must undergo six months of vocational training at Madhuban before they're allowed to apprentice on a real logging operation. During their stay, they are taught everything they need to know about working in the jungle. "Most of the elephants are born in Bihar state," said Abdul Razak, the school's director and veterinarian. "We bring them over by ship from the mainland and teach them several skills including pushing logs, dragging logs, and loading logs into the back of a truck. By the time they leave this school, they must know about 25 commands in Hindi."

Leaving the elephants behind, Forbes charted a course to the northeast. On the horizon we could see our next destination, the swarthy outline of Havelock Island. Prior to World War II the island was uninhabited, but in the years since Indian independence

This elderly islander is a resident of Diglipur, the largest town on North Andaman. Cricket action (opposite) hits fever pitch in a match between two school teams at Mayabandar on Middle Andaman. The sport is a holdover from British colonial days.

Havelock has been opened to settlers from the mainland. These are mostly Bengalis, who live much as they did back on the mainland: In thatched-roof houses with dirt floors, guided by a seasonal cycle of farmwork and religious festivals—and in the early days nearly as isolated from the modern world as the aboriginal tribes on nearby islands.

WE DROPPED ANCHOR off Radhanagar Beach, a crescent of ivory sand that is well on its way to becoming one of those mythical stops along the Hippie Trail—a place where certain young Western travelers find their Asian nirvana. The strand looked deserted, but peering through binoculars I spotted people among the trees in various states of undress ranging from loincloths and sarongs to completely naked.

Ian and I hit the beach with a thud, crashing through the surf in an outboard dinghy piloted by a young crewman from the *Tanveer.* We were soon engaged in conversation with the local pilgrims. A German woman, blue-eyed and blond, explained how she and three companions had been camped at Radhanagar for ten days, cooking over an open fire and sleeping in hammocks strung between the tree trunks. A group of Australians complained about dogs

filching food from their tent, but with that off their chest they began to extol the virtues of paradise.

Farther up the beach we stumbled onto an elderly Indian gentleman who had established an open-air shop to serve the visitors. He was sitting bare-chested, a machete perched on his lap, reading the *Bhagavad Gita*. But he quickly sprang to life as we approached. "You want coconut?" he asked. He snatched a ripe fruit and swung his machete into whacking position.

We met an older British woman who had been traveling in India. "This is my last stop—two weeks on Havelock," she said with a long sigh. "Each day I find some little gem. A bay with a white-sand beach, a new place to snorkel." She had found the end of her rainbow and didn't want to leave.

Sailing around the western shore, we made for Havelock's main jetty, a sleepy seaside village called Lapcum that is more commonly called Number One because it is the starting point of the island's single road. All the local villages boast two names. Govindnagar, the market town, is also called Number Three because it lies three kilometers from the jetty. Vijaynagar, location of the solitary hotel, is also Number Five.

Everyone was getting ready for the impending Hindu Holi Festival—an annual holy day associated with Lord Krishna and something of a harvest festival in the more tropical parts of India. Bengali settlers at Number Five invited us to join their Holi festivities. That night the holiday literally exploded into action with a giant bonfire to celebrate the end of harvest and drive evil spirits from the village. Villagers erected a hut from dried banana leaves—representing the house where

Lalaji Bay on the eastern shore of Long Island is one of dozens of pristine beaches that garnish the Andamans. The only development here is a small coconut plantation.

the local demoness lives—and we crouched inside, huddled together in the dark. Someone set fire to the outside of the hut, and one by one we dashed through the doorway as the structure went up in flames. The last one out, a lanky teenage boy, was hailed as the bravest person in the village.

As embers floated into the full-moon sky, we joined the villagers in a feast made up entirely of foods they had harvested themselves: Steamed rice cut into neat squares, which we ate off banana-leaf plates, followed by coconuts, papayas, and other tropical fruits. Dessert was raw sugarcane and various supersweet baked treats.

Next morning, Captain Forbes set a course through a knot of largely uninhabited islands to the north of Havelock. Most still bear their original British colonial names: Peel, Wilson, Nicholson, Outram, and the two Lawrences (John and Henry). For

the first time since leaving Port Blair we were moving through pristine wilderness—mangrove swamps and rain forest that are virtually unchanged from when the first Europeans sailed this way.

I SAT IN THE BOW and watched the wild islands. There are few places with a more twisted history—abounding in tales of shipwrecks, savages, and cannibalism. The name Andaman is thought to derive from Hanuman, the monkey god of the *Ramayana* epic, who according to legend used the islands as stepping stones between India and Sri Lanka. But the Andamans were also called Timai Thevu (Islands of Impurity) because of the natives' supposed taste for human flesh.

Put off by this fearsome reputation, mariners shunned the Andamans until the late 18th century. Lt. Archibald Blair of the Royal Navy was dispatched to the islands in 1789 to survey local waters and start a settlement, which was abandoned in 1796 largely because of an outbreak of disease. The penal colony was established in 1858, and for nearly a century the Andamans served as the Devil's Island of British India. Following the Indian Mutiny of 1857, Port Blair and environs were flooded with political rabble-rousers from the mainland.

Only after independence did the penal role decline in favor of logging and fishing. Now the Indian government is looking beyond primary production, to an era when they hope the local economy will be propelled by trade and tourism. There is talk of turning Port Blair into a free-trade zone like Hong Kong, and of transforming the entire Andaman chain into an Indian Ocean version of the Caribbean, with cruise ships, luxury resorts, and an airport that can handle jumbo jets. But all it is right now is talk. Which means that places such as Lalaji Bay, our next destination, will remain secluded and unspoiled well into the future.

Lalaji lies on the eastern flank of Long Island, a dazzling strand backed by coconut palms. Nestled in the coconut grove were the modest huts of plantation workers and their families. Total population: ten. The foreman's name was Malandi and he seemed delighted by our arrival. "Our last visitors were three months ago," he said.

Despite the solitude, Malandi figured life was pretty good at Lalaji Bay. He spent his time harvesting coconuts and tending to other plantation chores. "The only bad thing is communication,"

he lamented. There was no telephone, radio, or television. No newspapers or magazines. The only link to the outside world was by trekking to a settlement on the western shore of Long Island, and that was usually impossible during the rainy season. Which prompted a question: What do you do when you're not working? Malandi flashed a toothless smile: "I round up cows and goats along the beach."

Sure enough, a cow was reclining in the cool surf, waves lapping over her back. She didn't bat an eyelid as I ambled past with my snorkel and fins, headed for the nearby reef. Within minutes of slipping into the water I had spotted at least a dozen varieties of tropical fish—black-and-yellow angels hovering around the branches of staghorn coral, clown fish hiding among the green fingers of sea anemones, parrot fish, surgeonfish, and giant clams with lips of lapis blue and royal purple.

THE SUN WAS SETTING over Middle Andaman as ML *Tanveer* sidled up to Rangat Jetty. The town itself was a 30-minute taxi drive to the west. Rangat is the second largest town in the Andamans, a thriving plywood center on the edge of the forest with a surprisingly large Christian population.

Hundreds of people were milling around Rangat's bazaar, eating in outdoor cafés and browsing through the merchandise of dimly lit shops. Hindi music poured from open windows, and every so often my eye caught the flicker of a sari or turban. Ian and I booked a room in the public works bungalow overlooking the bazaar, secured the services of a local guide, and headed up the coast to Cuthbert Bay.

An hour later we drove into a tiny fishing village called Panchavati. The

His head and hands smothered in a scarlet powder called gulaal, *a youth celebrates the annual festival of Holi at Number Five village on Havelock Island.*

fishermen and their families were already asleep, curled beneath blankets in front of their thatched shacks, as we crept past them to the beach. The moon had just risen, an orange blob on the eastern horizon, and a high tide was pounding against the beach—ideal conditions for observing sea turtles laying their eggs in the sand.

Walking north along the beach, we trekked miles without the faintest trace of a turtle. We were ready to turn back when Ian suddenly spotted flipper marks in the sand. Following the tracks we found a Ridley turtle, moaning and groaning with all her might as she struggled to dig a pit in the sand. Dropping her eggs—some 60 soft, white orbs each about the size of a Ping-Pong ball—she went scrambling back into the waves.

Early the following morning we set sail again, gliding along the eastern flank of Middle Andaman. It was a gorgeous

day, bright blue and not a cloud in the sky. As Forbes stood on the bridge, wheel in hand, he described his long-standing love affair with the islands. "I first came to the Andamans as a schoolboy, to visit my sister in Port Blair. I never wanted to go back home to Bombay, and as soon as I finished school I moved here permanently. That was 1970. I thought it was paradise—so much green, so much water, so much open space after Bombay. I've never had the desire to leave."

Yet now that very possibility was looming on his horizon. His mother and sister had moved to Australia years before. They were sponsoring his immigration, urging Forbes to leave the turmoil of India behind. "I don't know," he said in a troubled voice. "We'll have to see what happens. The family thinks

it's quite strange that I don't jump at the chance of going to Australia. But why leave paradise?"

Yet paradise was changing. As Forbes went on to explain, the Andamans were in a period of transition. Businessmen were grabbing for land. Some officials were turning a blind eye to illegal logging and animal poaching. Politicians were trying to pad the election rolls by sponsoring thousands of new settlers. Those settlers, in turn, were encroaching on tribal lands and ravaging the rain forest to make way for farms. "I don't hold out much hope," he concluded. "So many people covet the land for timber, farming, fishing. I don't think there'll be much left in another ten years."

Our next port of call was Mayabandar, an old town perched on a ridge between the open ocean and a mangrove swamp. There is only one street, flanked by pastel office buildings and wooden bungalows with pretty gardens. The inhabitants are a mixed bag: A few convict progeny, Karen tribespeople from Burma, and Bengali refugees from Bangladesh, all of which endows the town with a decidedly exotic atmosphere.

Not far from Mayabandar, in a tiny village called Govindpur, we chanced upon a Krishna chanting festival, a

Aberdeen Bazaar is today the commercial hub of Port Blair, the Andaman capital. Most shops, once run by the descendants of criminals and political prisoners, have been taken over by Tamil immigrants. In 1859, the biggest battle between British troops and aboriginal warriors was fought at the then settlement of Aberdeen.

marathon event that runs around the clock for three days. Hundreds of devotees, including 11 chanting teams, had gathered outside a shrine. Each team takes center stage for 90 minutes, the chanters starting slowly but gradually working themselves into a trancelike frenzy of singing, dancing, and prayer. We watched from the sidelines as one group reached its celestial climax. Some of the chanters passed out, and others burst into uncontrollable tears, clutching other members of the congregation.

The wind kicked up and the sea was rough leaving Mayabandar, but after sunset the water turned as smooth as glass again. It was pitch dark, a million stars above and dolphins leaping on

either side of the bow. All of a sudden, a slice of light appeared on the eastern horizon. I thought it was lightning at first, a far-off thunderstorm. But the slice kept rising and expanding until a harvest moon was perched above the sea. It was one of those perfect moments that travelers rave about—and wouldn't trade for all the money in the world.

We slept on deck that night and woke with the sun the following morning. My eyes slid open to the sight of a banded sea snake slithering up a dock and disappearing into a dark hole. On the other side of the deck, the water was filled with green fish with pink snouts and turquoise fins. A sea eagle soared high above, searching for its breakfast. Wiping the sleep from my eyes, I stood up and gazed around. We were docked at Ariel Jetty on North Andaman, on the edge of a vast natural bay called Port Cornwallis, the northern extremity of our journey.

Ian and I took an early morning bus into Diglipur, the only proper town on North Andaman. The bus was crowded with schoolchildren in neat uniforms and housewives with empty baskets tucked beneath their arms, headed for the morning market. Thick mist hung over the Diglipur valley as we pulled into the market square.

After checking into the works department bungalow, we begged a jeep off the executive engineer and explored deep into the countryside. There were hundreds of pocket-size rice farms, carved from virgin forest over the past 20 years: thatched-roof homesteads on the edge of civilization, islands of human hope in the middle of a vast wilderness.

Later that day, Ian went in search of

photo opportunities, and I spent a long time walking along Ramnagar Beach south of Diglipur. The strand was at least a half mile long, backed by rain forest and protected by a thick coral reef. It was a beautiful spot, but best of all, I was alone. Only my footprints in the sand. Only my splashing in the surf. Only my eyes on the reef. I had reached the end of my own particular trail and slipped into a profound sense of calm that few places on this earth can induce.

THE FOLLOWING WEEK we were back in Port Blair, unpacking our bags from the ML *Tanveer* and bidding adieu to Captain Forbes. Soon it would be time to fly back to the Indian mainland.

But there was unfinished business. Anstice Justin had recently returned from his journey into hostile tribal country, and we were eager to learn what he had discovered. "The contact mission was only partially successful," he said. "We were not able to establish contact with the Jarawa who are responsible for the attacks. We were on the beach for more than three hours and saw no one."

But things had gone much better on North Sentinel Island. The government group had lured the people from their jungle hideout by offering coconuts and bananas (having never been settled, Sentinel has no cultivated fruit trees). At that point, Justin and the others were allowed to come ashore and explore two Sentinelese villages.

He was extremely excited about what they had found: Dugout canoes, cooking vessels, food storage areas, as well as plastic items and plywood that had washed up on the beach and been adapted by the Sentinelese to various

The morning catch comes ashore at Dugnabad Cove in Port Blair. Among the species that thrive here are tuna, grouper, snapper, mackerel, and shark. The rich fisheries cause friction between the Indian Navy and boats that stray into Indian territorial waters from neighboring countries.

everyday uses. Pig jaws had been hung under the roofs of their huts as hunter's trophies.These are the kind of items that would delight any anthropologist.

Among other objects sighted on the contact mission was an iron beam, perhaps from a shipwreck, that Justin thinks they use as an anvil. But there is disagreement among anthropologists as to whether the people know how to work metal with heat. They do use metal heads for arrows and harpoons.

Several days later, I left the Andamans. As the plane rose above the Bay of Bengal, we passed North Sentinel Island. I found myself wondering if the tribal people were watching, hidden in the jungle, gazing skyward at the big silver bird. It was somehow a comforting thought—that there are still people from a different millennium inhabiting these islands. But at the same time I knew the clock was ticking: The 20th century might be their last.

Coconuts plucked amid the ruins on Ross Island (above) are loaded on a long boat, called a "country boat," to be sold at markets in nearby Port Blair. With an ease that belies the difficulty of his daily work, a coconut harvester (opposite) scales a tree at Burmanallah on South Andaman. Many of the villagers there are Christians who immigrated from Kerala state on the mainland. They make rope from coconut husks and dry the oil-bearing meat in the sun to sell as copra.

Hoping to tempt the Holi Festival crowds, a banana farmer pushes his heavily laden bike toward the open-air market in Number Three village on Havelock Island.

Following pages: A lateen-rigged fishing boat plies the Andaman Sea off North Point on South Andaman.

Nearly everyone in the Andamans comes from somewhere else in India, forming a tranquil amalgam of the nation's various ethnic and religious groups. Tamil youths (below) water vegetable crops on the outskirts of Austinabad, a settlement south of Port Blair on South Andaman. Two generations of a Bengali family (opposite) perform their morning ablutions near Lapcum Harbor on Havelock Island. Most of the original settlers on this island were Bengalis from the mainland.

A *young girl clutches her mother's hand at the Krishna chanting festival in Govindpur on Middle Andaman.*

Following pages: Bearing fresh water from a nearby well, a woman heads back to Durgapur, a fishing village near Ariel Bay on North Andaman. Ariel Bay marks the northern limit of settlement in the Andamans; beyond lies nothing but rain forest and the open ocean.

PITC

AND
NORFOLK

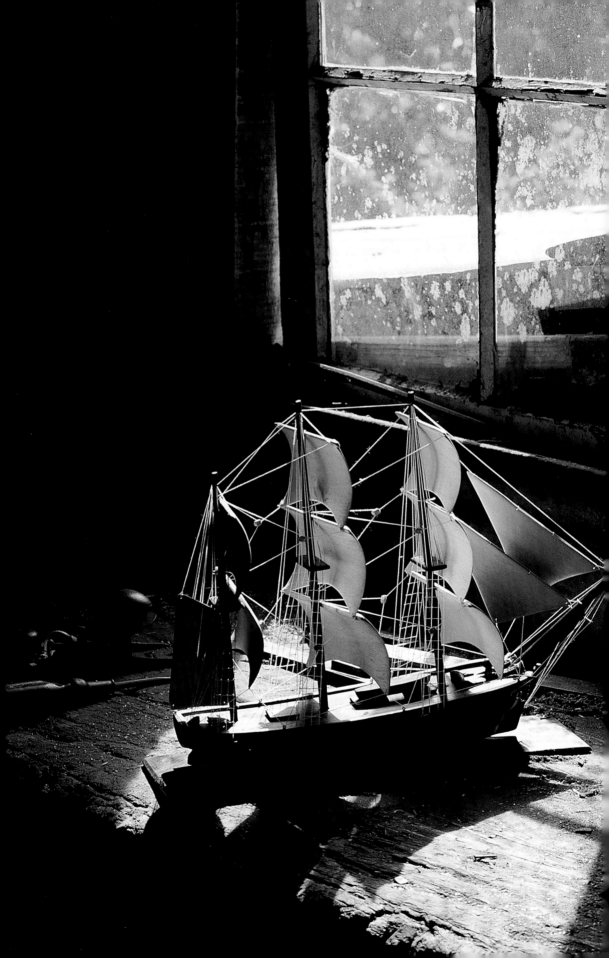

Pitcairn and Norfolk

By Simon Winchester

Photographs by R. Ian Lloyd

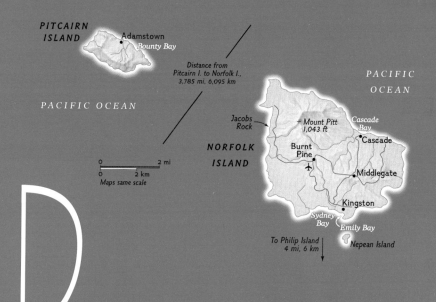

PITCAIRN ISLAND
Adamstown
Bounty Bay

Distance from Pitcairn I. to Norfolk I., 3,785 mi, 6,095 km

PACIFIC OCEAN

PACIFIC OCEAN

0   2 mi
0   2 km
Maps same scale

Jacobs Rock

NORFOLK ISLAND

Mount Pitt 1,043 ft

Cascade Bay
Cascade

Burnt Pine

Middlegate

Kingston

Sydney Bay
Emily Bay

To Philip Island 4 mi, 6 km
Nepean Island

IVIDED BY THOUSANDS OF MILES OF WARM PACIFIC SEAS, YET TWINNED ETERNALLY BY THE VAGARIES OF HISTORY, THE OLD BRITISH ISLAND COLONIES OF PITCAIRN AND NORFOLK SLUMBER ON, HALF OBLIVIOUS TO THE MODERN WORLD. THEY PRESERVE REMINDERS OF ONE OF THE MOST FAMOUS NAVAL MUTINIES OF ALL TIME.

HMS Bounty *model sits on the workbench of a Pitcairn descendant of Fletcher Christian. Preceding pages: A Pitcairn longboat slices ocean rollers at Adamstown's tiny harbor.*

*C*lad in the same style as their Victorian predecessors (glasses and wristwatches aside), Norfolk residents wait in Kingston for the annual reenactment of the landing of the Pitcairn Islanders. The entire community of 194 arrived at the abandoned penal settlement of Norfolk on June 8, 1856.

Following pages: Sturdy in its isolation, a tree on a Kingston knoll overlooks barren Philip Island, named for a British governor.

The little room was tense and still, bathed in a deafening hiss of static. Outside was as hot as only California's Central Valley knows heat: Endless walnut orchards, orange groves, and grapevines burned in the scalded and unmoving air. But inside the radio shack it was cool, the shelves of transmitters and amplifiers protected by powerful air conditioners from the furnace outside. Nothing moved, except for a small fly that buzzed irritatingly around and a red-numbered clock that soundlessly ticked down the seconds.

THEN THE NUMBERS on the clock, representing Radio Time or Universal Time, tumbled over to zero hours, zero minutes, zero seconds, and in that same instant the static ended. It was replaced, but only for a second or two, by silence and then, faintly at first, by a warble of Morse code. Jules Wenglare, whose radio shack this was, suddenly attentive, sat forward to fine-tune his receiver, delicately twisting a wheel to the left and then to the right until the stream of code came in loud and undistorted. Satisfied, he sat back: "That's him," he said. "That's our Tom. Right on time."

The Morse stopped its warbling, and in its place boomed out a voice—a deep, rich voice, colored with an accent that sounded at once Australian and English, of an old-fashioned country kind: "This is VR6TC calling, VR6TC. Victor Romeo Six Tango Charlie." It was Tom Christian on Pitcairn Island in the Pacific Ocean, making contact with the outside world. Who would be listening this time?

Who is listening? Who knows we are here? Does somebody care? Questions like these have been asked repeatedly since that January day in 1790 when nine mutineers on Her Majesty's Ship *Bounty* ran the trackless wastes of the South Pacific and settled on the tiny mid-ocean volcanic island that had been named after Robert Pitcairn, the midshipman who first sighted it.

Communication has ever since been exceptionally difficult—the vast sea-distances that have left it an island without any real neighbors make sure of that. The stark reality of isolation has long since defined the island and its inhabitants. Over time, however, there has been a distinct sea change in what that isolation has meant.

Back in the early years it was seen as a boon, since the first islanders—on the run from the authorities—very much wanted to be left completely alone and unfound. Those few who are left on Pitcairn today—British colonial citizens all, inhabitants of what seems like an English village trapped in mid-ocean and in a two-century time warp—yearn for some connection with the world beyond. The radio is their main link.

Thirty-six people—the figure has fluctuated somewhat over recent years—cling gamely on in this sole remaining British outpost in the South Pacific Ocean. Theirs is a unique situation: They live in perhaps the most lonely settlement on the planet, imprisoned by distance and pinioned by their history.

Legally the colony comprises four

islands: Pitcairn itself, the only populated possession, whose occupants all live in the tiny capital of Adamstown halfway up the volcano's side; the flat-topped limestone knoll of Henderson Island, 104 miles away; and two isolated coral atolls, Oeno and Ducie, 74 miles north and 291 miles east respectively. London's interest in her tiny faraway fly-speck of real estate is these days minimal. The Governor of Pitcairn lives far off in New Zealand and visits the island only once every couple of years. Few other British officials ever go. Little tax money has been spent on improving the lot of the people. A satellite phone and fax went in three years ago, mainly for emergencies.

As a consequence of their history and geography, the islanders' lives have evolved into a subtle compound of unusual factors. To a degree the 36 inhabitants exist in a tropical idyll—coconut palms blowing in the trade winds; blue seas brimming with fish; old British habits of common courtesy and afternoon tea and cricket games played in a mountain meadow. But the circumstances of the place have added other factors as well—a chronic poverty (borne with great dignity); an unquestioning loyalty to Britain (though few have ever been there); a staunch Christian piety (which is a result of the energetic mission work of 19th-century American visitors of the Seventh-day Adventist persuasion).

On a day-to-day basis, the islanders work at their vegetable patches; they raise goats and chickens; they collect mangoes and oranges and pineapples; they fish; they watch out for passing ships. In Adamstown's little square, a great anchor from the *Bounty* rusts slowly outside in the damp heat, and Fletcher Christian's old Bible stands unguarded in a glass case in the church—everyone and everything seems to drowse in the eternal sun.

The chubby old ladies of the community, respected in the way of most Pacific peoples, snooze peacefully on the town bench or wave languidly at passersby. Every so often the peace is broken by the buzz saw din of one of the little red Honda motor-tricycles that many people now use to negotiate the muddy roadways. Those who don't have them complain mildly about the noise, the ugly sound of Progress. Until the late 1960s, except for the boats and two tractors, one with a bulldozer blade, that carved out some of the roads, there wasn't an engine in the place.

In Pitcairn, people seem always to be waiting and hoping—hoping most of all for the tolling of the old ship's bell that speaks of a ship spotted on the horizon and the possibility of contact with new people, some selling of stamps and miro-wood carvings, the makings of a busy and maybe even profitable day.

THE RADIO OPERATOR—perhaps Tom Christian, perhaps his wife, or one of the old ladies called up to duty—twiddles the dials and calls out the plaintive question that has become a Pitcairn cliché, a query well known to mariners in these South Sea shipping lanes: "You will be stopping?" the operator's voice sings out over the air. "Won't you?"

More often than not, the answer is, "No, sorry to say, not this time." The California radio ham does his best to see that some vessels do stop. His weekly conversations sometimes include the Pitcairners' shopping list—ordinary things such as batteries, garden seeds,

peanut butter, jeans. He buys supplies from his hometown Kmart, mails them down to a shipping company in Houston, and the bosses there see that their next New Zealand-bound vessel heaves to briefly off Pitcairn and delivers the goods. Pitcairn radio offers the islanders such news as this and maybe the bonus of a cruise liner that plans to drop by for a day with its hundreds of dollar-bearing passengers. But mostly it brings regrets from ships that say they are in too much of a rush to stop.

It was long before the invention of radio that the first settlers came to Pitcairn, and they spent their initial years on the island doing their best to hide. The circumstances leading up to their arrival are well known: the infamous naval mutiny, an ugly event made more famous by three big Hollywood films.

All the stagings commemorate the event itself and its curious aftermath, and all memorialize the men and machinery caught up in it—principal among them being the anti-heroic figure of Lt. William Bligh, the romancer-mutineer Fletcher Christian, and the breadfruit-laden converted warship, the *Bounty*.

She was the HMS *Bethia* before she was dispatched to Tahiti to collect breadfruit seedlings and transport them to Caribbean plantations, to provide food for the local slaves. It was as the *Bounty*—renamed for the bounty she was carrying—that this 91-foot vessel sailed from Spithead, with 44 crewmen under the command of 33-year-old Lieutenant Bligh and with 24-year-old Mr. Christian as mate.

This pair of seamen—whom history has linked forever—left England on December 23, 1787, as firm friends; they parted company off Tofua on April 28, 1789, as sworn and bitter enemies. Few will forget Charles Laughton's defiant shout to Clark Gable, in the 1935 film, as the great ship moved away from Bligh and his 18 loyalists, whom the mutineers had cast adrift in their tiny pinnace: "I will see you *hang*, Mr. Christian!"

But he never did. Bligh got to London and instigated a hunt for the mutineers; three were sent to the gallows. But not Fletcher Christian. By that time Christian was well established on uninhabited Pitcairn Island and beginning one of the strangest colonial sagas ever known.

RAISING PITCAIRN after a long sea journey is an unforgettable experience, doubtless much the same today as it was when Christian's men finally came across the island on January 15, 1790. They did so partly as a result of an earlier mariner's error, for when Christian sailed the *Bounty* to the place where the charts said Pitcairn was, they found the sea quite empty: Capt. Philip Carteret of HMS *Swallow*, the first discoverer, had made a major navigation mistake. But Christian saw swiftly how this could aid his fugitive plans: The charts of his pursuers, he realized, would be wrong as well, and providing he could eventually find Pitcairn himself (as he did, 200 miles away from where it was mapped), he would have the advantage of being on what was essentially a lost island—the perfect hideaway.

The charts are better now, of course, and when I first saw the island from the bridge of a New Zealand warship one April morning more than two centuries later, it lay exactly where we had expected it to be—a couple of degrees south of the Tropic of Capricorn, more or less halfway along an imaginary line drawn between Panama and New Zealand. It was a sight I have never forgotten: A brilliant green pyramid rising with forbidding abruptness from the endless expanse of open sea—an island that looked more lonely than it is possible to imagine.

"You will be stopping here at Pitcairn, won't you?" I heard the island radio operator ask the famous question. Her voice had a note of anxious expectancy. She had a strange, soft accent: She called her island "Peet-kern," with a lilt and a pleasant sibilance. We assured her that we were indeed planning to stop. We would remain, we said, for some little while.

From a distance there was little to see, other than cliffs and thick green vegetation and hills with palms and occasional tropical pines. The island looked almost deserted, and our close approach to the steep cliffs and sharp rocks of the island shore was every bit as risky and unnerving as it must have seemed to the crew of the *Bounty*.

We stopped and dropped anchor outside the bay, just as the *Bounty* had done. Our expectancy—on being able to land on an island still known to so few today—must very nearly have matched Fletcher Christian's. He is recorded as going on a brief reconnoiter and returning "with a joyful expression such as we had not seen on him for a long time past"; the island was uninhabited, though Polynesians had clearly been there at one time, since breadfruit and bananas and coconut palms had been planted. The mutineers and their companions—Tahitian women and a few men—were to disembark at last and begin the formidable business of establishing a brand new settlement, out in the middle of nowhere.

So the men and women landed at Bounty Bay, as we did and as all other visitors do today. (A year-old baby, who had been born on Tahiti, was said to have been floated ashore in a barrel.) The men and women hauled their goods up what they called the Hill of Difficulty, much as we did. They set up camp on The Edge, where Pitcairn's capital, Adamstown, still huddles among wild rose apple shrubs and groves of pines.

But then there was a difference. Whereas today's visitors keep their boats firmly and proudly anchored offshore— to show, as we did, that *they have made it*—Christian ordered all sign of his own ship erased, forever. The settlers spent a week stripping the old *Bounty* of every potentially useful piece of hardware. From the vessel they took the sails for making camp, the oak timbers for permanent houses, the nails for building, the galley kettles for cooking stew. They also took every living thing, every goat, chicken, pig, and dog—but these last were drowned when Christian realized their barking might be heard by a passing ship. Then the little vessel was burned to the waterline. It was a sad but very necessary precaution, "to remove her giveaway silhouette…for Eternity."

There were 28 settlers in all: the 9 mutineers, 6 Tahitian men and 12

British missionaries built St. Barnabas Chapel (left) on Norfolk in 1880, and young and old still worship there. Proud Norfolk owner Baker McCoy (right) displays the surviving example of two wooden tablets carved with the Ten Commandments by John Adams, the longest Bounty *survivor on Pitcairn.*

women, and the babe-in-arms-in-a-barrel, called Sully; and they all took themselves up to The Edge. They made an interesting ethnic mélange, but one that was bound to rupture under the stresses of isolation, jealousy, racial rivalry, and strong drink—which a Scotsman, Mr. McCoy, found he could distill from the roots of the ti plant.

It was by violent means that, one by one, the men died. One went berserk with drink and was killed by two of the others in self-defense. McCoy, the distiller, jumped off a cliff with a rock tied round his neck. The Polynesians, angered over Fletcher Christian's decision not to allow them to own Pitcairn land, murdered him (although

some do say Christian managed to get away from the island, was spotted in a London street, and died peacefully in England's Lake District). Arguments over women resulted in the death of four others, Messrs. Martin, Mills, Brown, and Williams, who betimes had done away with all the Tahitian men too. And then Edward Young, the *Bounty*'s midshipman, died of asthma.

An American sealer named Mayhew Folger next arrived at Pitcairn in 1808, 18 years after the mutiny. He stopped his vessel, the *Topaz*, to check on what he supposed to be an unpeopled island.

Australian novelist Colleen McCullough, author of The Thorn Birds, *makes her home on Norfolk. The marble bust reflects her new literary interest in the Roman Empire.*

What he discovered on shore enthralled him. There, one man presided benignly over a group of women and children. This was the sole surviving mutineer: "Reckless Jack" Adams, the *Bounty*'s barely literate able seaman, now a devout, Bible reading, patriarchal elder, who appeared to be taking sedulous care of the 10 Polynesian women and 23 children who made up the rest of Pitcairn's population. Adams was a model of virtue and piety, as was his flock: All prayed, shared everything, and seemingly loved one another.

And, most incredible of all to a sealing captain who had come 10,000 miles from his home into seas where there was much hostility and little comprehension: The islanders—one Briton and 33 of Polynesian or mixed stock—all spoke English. A speck of a volcano in mid-Pacific, and the population read the Good Book and spoke the language of the King!

John Adams being so mild and so pious, later visitors from the Royal Navy, armed with the power to seize him, could not bring themselves to arrest him. Eventually he died of natural causes.

In 1838 the island was incorporated into the empire. During the 1820s, new settlers had arrived—a Bristol shipwright named Buffett; a Welshman named Evans; and Nobbs, the bastard son of a marquess. The weather and crops fluctuated, and with them the size of the population and its health. At one time the numbers grew to the barely supportable figure (given that Pitcairn is only two miles long and one wide) of more than 220.

And therein lay the seeds of a second sea change in the island's fortunes and the beginning of the links that Pitcairn was forced to make with another island, one of which the islanders were all quite ignorant and which lay 3,785 miles away to the west in the Coral Sea.

At about the same time that Fletcher Christian and his outlaw followers were beginning their settlement on Pitcairn, the first of thousands of miserable British transported prisoners were beginning theirs—under far more rigorous conditions—on this other island, which was also British, and which had been named, in honor of a celebrated duchess of the time, Norfolk Island. Norfolk had been discovered by Captain Cook in 1774, seven years after Carteret had first seen Pitcairn. The histories of the two islands have since proceeded in a kind of South Pacific lockstep, with uncanny parallels and coinciding fortunes.

NORFOLK IS RATHER BIGGER than Pitcairn, though still only five miles by three. Like Pitcairn it had no native population at the time of its discovery by Cook, although old, overgrown plantations of yams and bananas, and the presence of some rock tools, suggested someone had lived there once. Physically the island is in many ways similar to Pitcairn. It is volcanic by geology and subtropical by climate, and so it, too, is green and brimming with lush vegetation. Its only native mammal, a bat, is thought to be extinct; and its birdlife, free from predators, is abundant. There is a volcano, Mount Pitt, and scores of lower hills, on all of which grows the peculiarly configured, ramrod-straight evergreen known around the world as the Norfolk Island pine. "Here then is a nother Isle where Masts for the largest Ships may be had," wrote Cook in his dispatch to the Admiralty. He promptly claimed it.

Ideal a place though Norfolk may have seemed then to Cook, and pretty a place though it appears to the tourist thousands who now visit each year, its early history was of barbarism beyond belief. For while Pitcairn was chosen as a place of voluntary self-exile by criminals on the run, Norfolk was settled as a place of involuntary exile for criminals. His Majesty's government in London declared that Norfolk—like the then colony of New South Wales— be used as a penal colony, a secure mid-ocean lockup.

But in 1856 came the event that was to join the two islands forevermore. Pitcairn was by then full to bursting, and there had been a rash of poor harvests and a scarcity of fish; food was running low. The islanders petitioned London to find them another island home. It should be large enough and more suitable to the islanders' needs. It only had to be in the same ocean and be able to sustain the same kind of crops the islanders could manage.

London, which lately had been shamed by criticism of the terrible conditions at the prison on Norfolk, decided that Norfolk would be ideal. The colonial authorities ordered the jails closed and the inmates shipped off to Tasmania. They took a vote among the Pitcairners that resulted in a nearly five to one majority in favor of moving; finally all agreed to go. Then they hired the passenger vessel *Morayshire*, loaded the entire population of Pitcairn—193 men, women, and children—and sailed them westward to Norfolk.

On June 8, 1856, the party—its numbers increased by the arrival en route of the infant Reuben Denison Christian—arrived in Kingston; with the settling of the 194 Pitcairners on Norfolk, the link that has since secured the two islands together was firmly forged.

Each June that arrival is fully and formally reenacted. The ceremony is performed with a solemnity that says much about the subtle complications of Norfolk's present condition. Islanders gather on Kingston's little pier in the morning, all of them dressed in the clothes they would have worn a century and a half before—the men barefoot and in straw hats with white tapa shirts and their linen trousers held up by black suspenders, the women in long skirts and shawls, the smaller children pushed in carriages lined with banana leaves and decorated with flowers.

Those allowed to take part in the landing party are from the eight families who are formally recognized as Norfolk's Pitcairn descendants: families called Adams, Christian, McCoy, Quintal, and Young (sprung from the actual mutineers), and families called Buffett, Evans, and Nobbs (descendants of the Pitcairn settlers of later times). The Norfolk telephone book has no fewer than 37 Christians, many of them sporting nicknames—Toofy, for instance, or Loppy, or Bodge—for which the people of both islands are renowned.

A few brave souls embark in a whaler and reenact the landing itself. All their kin watch apprehensively as the flimsy craft smashes through the heavy surf from the rollers that boom in from the ocean. The assembled throng is then greeted by the island's bearded Speaker of the Legislature, David Buffett, who leads the crowd up toward the capital and its tidy ranks of historic buildings.

They sing the national anthem, and their leaders lay wreaths on the war

A tramp steamer undertakes the risky business of unloading a new car onto a tender off Norfolk. Calm seas here are all too rare. Ships in passage between New Zealand and Australia call at the island only when powerful Pacific Ocean rollers allow their approach.

memorial. But it is not the Australian anthem they sing, as one would expect, since Norfolk is a territory under the authority of the Commonwealth of Australia. They sing "God Save the Queen." "We islanders are very proud of our imperial connections," says David Buffett, dressed in a British naval uniform of Victorian times. "This is not as Australian a place as the Australians would like to think."

AND THEREIN LIES one of the many oddities of an island that, more than most, has become curiously bound by its history. It is an oasis of Britishness, stiff with reminders of its colonial past, and yet officially it is no longer British at all,

but Australian. And there are further complications: Even an Australian needs a passport to visit Norfolk, and those who come to live there permanently (such as the noted *Thorn Birds* author, Colleen McCullough) have to win permission not from Australia but from the authorities on Norfolk. And yet, in this matter of immigration, and all others too, Canberra is the court of last resort. The Australian flag can be seen at least as often as the green-and-white pine-tree flag of the island, and the Australian dollar is the only currency.

Within the society of 1,800 people who now live on Norfolk, there are subtle divisions. Are you a Pitcairner? Is your name Buffett or Adams or Christian? Are you related by marriage? Can you claim any link, tenuous or not? Or are you a Johnny-come-lately—a mainlander—someone whose features lack the remnant Polynesian coloring that distinguishes the men and women who are properly descended from the mutineers and their fellow settlers?

"There is a pecking order here," said one islander, a woman not of Pitcairn descent. "Look at the rolls of those who work for the administration here, the government. They're all Pitcairners, every one." And when a small cargo ship called in at Sydney Bay a day or so

later and workers were summoned by radio to come and unload her, all were Pitcairners, by looks and by surname.

On Bounty Day the Pitcairners hold a huge lunch party inside the walls of the main prison. Long trestle tables are covered with the food that has emerged from the blending of Tahitian, English, Antipodean, and American whaler cuisine: Roast pigs; pies baked with periwinkles and eggs; trumpet fish baked in banana leaves; taro; three-finger poi; and great sticky puddings made of pineapple, coconut, yam, island sugar, honey, and boiled cream.

It is considered a great honor to be invited to break bread with one of the main family tables. Much of the talk is in "Norfolk," a curious language that has emerged over the years from the slow mixing of 18th-century English and Polynesian: *"Ah pik wan baket a'bibi,"* says a woman, telling how she got a bucket of periwinkles for her pie. *"Baes taim f'gu rama es sink saf,"* says another, confirming that the best time to get them from the beach is at low tide.

I mention to the speakers that I remember a similar language on Pitcairn itself. The women were startled and delighted. *"Yu bin Pitkern?"* they asked in a chorus, and pressed around when I said I had. *"Wats laik?"* I told them that

The venerable sport of lawn bowls, which has spoken of England and Empire since the time of Sir Francis Drake, remains an important part of Norfolk life. No distractions intrude on the studied calm of this Saturday game among members of the Norfolk Island Bowling Club at Burnt Pine.

I thought it a rather sad place, much neglected by the British, and that the remaining islanders—descendants of a small number who had gone back from Norfolk in the mid-19th century, and who were now mostly pious, nondrinking, nonsmoking followers of the Seventh-day Adventist church—had been forgotten by almost everyone. Adamstown, with its tumbled buildings and peeling paint and atmosphere of tropical decay, seemed to me—perhaps unkindly—a bit dilapidated.

"Demtal dem haapi sekam deswe," said one listener. The Pitcairners would like to come over to Norfolk to live. They wish their ancestors had never left. No, retorted another. *"Dem naewa gwena liiw Pitkern."* They'll never leave.

But later that afternoon, over at the far side of the prison-compound picnic, I found a smiling lad named Trent Christian, whom I had met on Pitcairn before, and whose parents still lived there. He had abandoned Pitcairn and had come to live on Norfolk, and he told me that he found the life on this island much more nearly normal, at least for a youngster, than the life he left behind. "Boring," was the word he used to describe the lonely existence back in Adamstown. "Here is more fun. And here you can get away." As if to emphasize his point a jet soared up from the airport runway at the island's center. It was the Air New Zealand Boeing, off to Auckland and the real world.

THERE IS, SAD TO SAY, a feeling abroad that Pitcairn's days may be numbered. The British government clearly wants to get rid of its far-flung responsibility, and has gone so far as to advertise for some foreigner to go to live there and try to come up with a plan to breathe economic life into the tiny community. Everyone admits there can never be an airport, or a regular shipping line, or much of an economy beyond the sale of postage stamps and miro-wood carvings.

Some in London wish longingly for the likes of Smiley Ratliff to appear again. Ratliff was a larger-than-life figure, a coal-mining millionaire from Virginia, who back in the eighties asked if he might buy, or at least lease, the flat limestone island of Henderson nearby. He would build an airport, he said, and would live out his years there with a group of like-minded Virginians.

The British were ready to cut a deal,

until zoologists reminded the government of the existence of the flightless Henderson rail and of a fruit-eating pigeon—protected species. A disappointed Mr. Ratliff was told to look elsewhere. Had the deal gone through, people like Tom Christian ruefully recall, Pitcairn might by now have enjoyed a rudimentary air service, and an income. The only way to be guaranteed passage there nowadays is to charter a boat from the Gambier Islands—costly, time-consuming, and well beyond the islanders' paltry means. "That blessed rail!" Tom Christian remembers still.

Life is hard, and getting harder. It is possible, almost all agree, that the few Pitcairn Islanders who remain may one day simply give up the struggle. They may then opt to come to Norfolk and settle there. "They may find that life here is fast compared to life on Pitcairn, but they would be totally welcome," says David Buffett, in his capacity as Speaker. Those who have come to Norfolk in recent times have readily assimilated through the island's immigration laws.

On my final day in Norfolk, I thought I should try to speak to Pitcairn once again, by radio. An environmentalist named John Anderson, who runs a small business telling tourists some of the *Bounty* story, has a ham-radio schedule with the island once a week. I went to his shack on a cool and rainy evening and listened hard for the tell-tale signature of Tom Christian's Morse code. It came right on time. "This is VR6TC, Victor Romeo Six Tango Charlie"—Tom Christian on Pitcairn Island calling.

And I told him that we were here on Norfolk Island; that we had celebrated Bounty Day, and eaten roast pig and

A Norfolk Island pine stands sentinel at Jacobs Rock, a popular spot for sunset viewing.

Following pages: This rare, misty image of the island's harbor on Bounty Bay was made for a 1983 NATIONAL GEOGRAPHIC *story.*

FOLLOWING PAGES: MELINDA BERGE

periwinkle pie and *pilhai* and three-finger poi, and that all Norfolk remembered the day when the *Morayshire* landed here, nearly a century and a half ago. We listened for his reply.

It was very faint, and the static was terrible. "Didn't get much of that—didn't get much of that. It is very hot here today. Very hot. They say there's a ship coming next Thursday, a ship next Thursday. We hope it will stop. Things are very quiet over here, very quiet."

And then the signal faded away, and the hiss of atmospherics took over, and we listened for a few moments more before switching off the radios. Out there was silence, and whatever Tom Christian was saying wasn't getting through. Just as in Fletcher Christian's day, Pitcairn is a place where, by choice or circumstance, one comes to hide, to be blotted out from the recesses of public memory—to enjoy, or suffer, the trials of being forever forgotten.

The relentless power of the sea and crumbling relics of history underlie the story of Norfolk Island. The ocean thunders on the shore at Sydney Bay. Here islanders have preserved administrative buildings of the former British penal colony— as well as barracks and cellblocks—as a reminder of colonial barbarism.

F amed for its obscurity and isolation, Pitcairn Island, a 1.75-square-mile volcanic dot (below), is almost lost in the vastness of the South Pacific. Fewer than 40 people live there now. But back in 1856 there were nearly 200—far too many mouths for so small an island to feed. The entire community

emigrated to Norfolk Island, although some did not stay. In an annual reenactment of their arrival, rowers upend oars in a whaler flying the British Union Jack.

Following pages: Pitcairn descendants walk to the Norfolk cemetery in yearly commemoration of their forebears.

DAVID HISER

After the Bounty Day solemnities, celebrants feast (below) on such traditional dishes as periwinkle pie, tropical fish baked in banana leaves, and yam-and-pineapple pudding. The picnic is reserved for linear descendants of the Pitcairn Islanders and their guests. Australian government administrator Allen Kerr, in traditional colonial dress (right), announces the winners of the children's costume contest to an attentive gathering. The Speaker of the Norfolk Legislature, David Buffett (foreground, at left), wears a British naval uniform of a century and a half ago.

ostumed island children race in high-spirited fashion through the Government House gardens on Bounty Day. The annual celebrations reflect a respect for tradition and history among Norfolk's Pitcairn descendants and an island-wide affection for the British crown, despite the monarchy's waning popularity in the rest of Australia.

Following pages: Sunset illuminates a rocky stretch of Norfolk's northern coastline at Cascade Bay.

Gotland

By Patrick R. Booz

Photographs by Ira Block

R ICH IN HISTORY AND NATURE'S BOUNTY,
GOTLAND, LARGEST BALTIC SEA ISLAND, HAS STOOD FOR
CENTURIES AS A CULTURAL CROSSROADS. ITS LIMESTONE
CLIFFS, IDYLLIC FARMS, STONE WINDMILLS IN FLOWER-
FILLED FIELDS, AND CHURCH SPIRES CREATE A SETTING
FOR VIKING TREASURES AND A WALLED MEDIEVAL CITY.
HERE TIME DAWDLES, AND TRADITIONS LIVE ON.

Raukar, *eroded limestone pillars, shelter a harpist on the island of Fårö.*
Preceding pages: Flag-waving jesters and musicians celebrate Medieval Week.

A russ *pony gets a friendly hug at the annual roundup in the island's forested center. Poppies (below) and other blooms turn Gotland into an isle of flowers in summer.*

Following pages: Visby, City of Roses and Ruins, earns its nickname. Along Fiskargränd Street, roof-high rose bushes decorate house after house.

languorous three-hour sunsets.

From the waterfront I could make out Visby's "steps" as the ancient town climbed in three stages to its limestone plateau heights. Striding to the top step, I turned my head 180 degrees to take in this medieval marvel, an amazingly well-preserved walled city that in 1995 joined UNESCO's World Heritage List. Church ruins stood out white against the background of terracotta roofs. Visby's renowned roses caught the last sun and burst into luminous shades of blood red, pink, peach, and lemon as they climbed stairways, walls, and turrets.

During the town's 13th-century heyday, 13 great churches stood within the wall. Only one remains intact: St. Mary's, a masterpiece of medieval Gothic architecture, built of large blocks of limestone surmounted by gargoyles and proud wooden spires. At midnight I heard the church's chimes send sonorous clangs through the darkness.

Visby's houses of yellow, red, ocher, and white, crisscrossed with half-timber beams, rise up to enclose narrow streets. Nearly 200 stone buildings remain from the Middle Ages: Six- and seven-story warehouses with handsome stepped gables, merchants' homes with decorated facades, and many wooden structures from the 17th and 18th centuries. But Visby's dominant masterpiece is the wall, begun in the 13th century; two miles long, it stands more than 30 feet tall in many places. One early morning I weaved in and out of arched gateways, trying to count the wall's more than 40 watchtowers. Rounding a corner, I was struck full-face by a rich, yeasty aroma that transported me back to a time of homemade beer and brick-baked bread.

In search of the real Gotlandic beer, known as *dricke*, I traveled deep into

E

vening swallows wheeled through the open window of a church ruin, rising heavenward with the music. Inside a piano recital transfixed an audience, while on the soft grass old couples and children rested against the ancient stones to listen. I stared up at white cottony clouds drifting past the jagged remnants of St. Nicholas's Church and imagined a time long ago when Gregorian chants, not Debussy, filled the air on this island so rich in history and culture.

Earlier that day a thin, gray pencil line just above the watery horizon had announced the approach to the island of Gotland, an offshore county of Sweden. Glittering sea spray from the metallic blue Baltic struck the ship that carried me from the mainland, 55 miles away, and I reflected on the countless ships that had made this journey through time.

Gotland, almost exactly the same size as Rhode Island, is the Baltic Sea's largest island: 86 miles long, 31 miles at the widest point, tapered at both ends. Its northernmost point reaches nearly to the latitude of Juneau, Alaska, yet its mid-sea location and warm currents endow it with more sunshine than any other place in northern Europe. Flawless weather filled my days, and each evening saw rich, buttery light stream across the waves, illuminating the little county seat of Visby throughout the countryside to a pristine farmstead surrounded by enormous shade trees and a garden overflowing with flowers. Kjell Ekman met me with a crushing handshake. "Welcome! Welcome!" Handsome and relaxed in a sleeveless tunic, with silvery hair, full mustache, and large blue eyes, he told me his philosophy of beer: "The beer brings harmony to the hormones, it makes the blood rich and healthy. It will make you calm and full of big thoughts, and your dreams will be happy! But don't drink too much. It's like rich food, you don't want to spoil things."

Kjell took me to his beer-making shed and hopped around animatedly, poking and banging huge tubs, lovingly explaining his craft. "Now to the tasting," he called, leading me down a steep flight of stairs to a cool, dark cellar containing two oak barrels. The brew was good, with a complicated taste of smoke, sweetness, and bitterness—in all a heady mix. The strong flavor comes from smoked malt, while juniper berries add a special delicacy. People here love dricke, and drink it particularly in the summer, at Christmas, and at Easter. According to Kjell it has an aura that helps bind friends together.

THE NAME GOTLAND probably comes from an Old Norse word, got or gut, meaning "outflow of water"; the place was known as "isle of streams" in ancient, wetter times, when bogs, rivulets, lakes, and estuaries dominated. The island has risen six feet in the last thousand years, and much of the land has been drained for fields. Today, 10 percent of Gotland's 58,000 people are farmers, far more than the 3 percent on the Swedish mainland, and they carry on a proud, continuous tradition. Dan Carlsson, a geographer and historian

who has lived here for 20 years, explained: "In some places, such as Anga parish in the east, we have a continuity from the fourth century to today. Single farms then, single farms today, same landscape, same crops. Imagine! The landscape reveals it." Carlsson knows how to read a landscape. "Gotland is a tremendously rich island, alive with history if you have the eyes. It developed an independent peasant society, and many Gotlanders today know exactly the history and predecessors of their farmland, back 500 years and more. Society was loosely organized then—no villages, no aristocracy, no king—and the people are proud of this early Republic of Gotland. Farmers have always been the most important people here."

But farming alone was not enough to bring the island to greatness. These independent people turned to the sea and learned to use Gotland's strategic position at the heart of the Baltic to control the new East-West trade that came with the Viking Age, beginning around A.D. 800.

The term "Viking" has always conjured up in my mind visions of ruthless raiders attacking coastal settlements in their trademark square-rigged ships, and indeed the verb "viking" meant "to go a-plundering." I learned, however, that Gotland's Vikings were of a different, gentler sort. They were mariners and merchants, not pirates and pillagers. Gotland's main trading outpost stood at Novgorod in Russia, south of today's St. Petersburg. Western Europe's appetite for foreign goods included two particular items: the winter pelt of the gray squirrel—a fur

known as miniver—and beeswax for
the candles of Christendom. This thriving
trade came via Gotland, whose ships
sailed all the seas of the known world,
from the Mediterranean to the Black
and Caspian Seas, and up and down
the rivers of Russia. They tapped into
a network of trade that extended from
Russia to Central Asia and Africa and
brought back to their island home
treasure hoards and huge numbers of
silver coins—mostly from Arabia, but
also from England, Germany, and as far
away as Afghanistan and Uzbekistan.

As THE VIKING ERA FADED, the Baltic
saw the rise of the Hanseatic League,
an early European Union that stretched
from Belgium to Norway to Russia, with
some 200 member towns.

Visby's rise to preeminence among
these Hanseatic towns came in the 13th
century as German traders increasingly
moved in to share in Gotland's wealth.
Visby became one of the Baltic's largest
and richest cities. It was the merchants
of Visby who built the city wall, not just
to keep out invaders from the sea, but
to protect themselves from their island
neighbors and to collect customs. In
time the Germans actually took over
Gotlandic trading, making Visby the sole
port. Previously, more than 50 harbors
had existed and farmers could trade
overseas freely; their loss of livelihood
led to civil war in 1288, after which all
trade had to pass through Visby.

Gotland's golden years lasted until
the end of the 14th century. But even
before then, larger ships that could carry
more goods, particularly the Hanseatic
workhorse known as the cog, simply
bypassed Gotland. Reduction in

*The remnant fishing
village of Helgumannen on
Fårö retains its 19th-
century look. Farmers here
built tiny wooden houses
and became seasonal
fishermen, seeking cod and
herring as staples, flounder
and salmon as delicacies.*

agriculture caused by worsening climate,
and in shipping to and from Novgorod,
brought on a decline that was completed
by the invasion of the Danish king
Valdemar Atterdag in 1361. A terrible
slaughter took place just outside Visby.
I paced the fields in the shadow of the
great wall, picturing the peasant army
fighting for life and independence. After
the defeat, Gotland became a sovereign
island run by Danes.

Before this, however, medieval
wealth and pride united with religious
faith to create Gotland's glory: 92
magnificent stone churches, spread
throughout the countryside like small
cathedrals. These repositories of
medieval art and culture have stood
virtually unchanged for 700 years.
Superficially they seem similar, each
with a tall tower-steeple, clean lines,
and steep, Romanesque-style roof. But
a careful look reveals great diversity in
wall paintings, baptismal fonts, stained

glass, and skillful stone carvings. Gothic opulence adds to the grandeur.

As I entered the church at Ekeby, its high ceiling and lustrous wall paintings drew my eyes upward, and the rich smell of burning candles enveloped me in a 13th-century aura. At Martebo a votive ship under sail hangs from a high vault, seeking God's protection for Gotland sailors. And at Stånga, sculptures mounted on the church porch depict the biblical story of King Herod and the slaughter of Bethlehem's babies—only the soldiers are dressed in armor, wield medieval weapons, and wear huge helmets with eye slits and visors. Gotland's churches became welcome friends, and I often scanned the horizon for a familiar steeple.

On the rugged northeast coast, at Kyllaj, I visited a site famous for its association with Carl von Linné—better known to the world as Linnaeus, father of the classification system that assigns a

Latin genus and species name to every plant and creature on earth. In the summer of 1741 he made a circuit of Gotland looking for economically useful plants, usually staying in a vicarage each evening and squeezing every piece of island information he could out of his hosts. Here, however, he stayed in the large country house of a wealthy local resident, which still stands as a museum of 18th-century life. He delighted in the grotesque limestone columns that surround the site and has left an amusing drawing of these monoliths—known as *raukar*—which have become emblematic of Gotland's coastal regions. He drank from a spring amidst the stone towers. I found his source, still known as Linnaeus's Well, and swallowed a mouthful of the cool water, mentally honoring the man who was fascinated by so many things here: Exploration, seal hunting, lime production, folk medicine, language, local customs and superstitions, farming methods, artifacts, even architecture and the making of roofs. Now, two and a half centuries later, I marveled at how much remained intact on Gotland.

In July the island erupts in color. Poppies paint fields red, rape flowers spread blinding sheets of yellow, wheat stands golden, and Gotland's champion provincial flower, *blåeld,* or blue fire, mantles entire landscapes with soft, purplish blue.

In the south-central part of the island, scents of sun-soaked earth mingled with pines and junipers, and I followed alleys of wildflowers down to pastures full of *russ* horses. This ancient breed—distant relatives of Iceland's famed ponies—now numbers about 500 on Gotland; only 70 remain wild, a reminder of the time a hundred years ago when the local people hunted and lassoed them for eating. Now they roam safe and healthy: solid, stocky little creatures of varying shades of brown, chestnut, and gray. Only children ride them, and today they are treated with great care and affection.

BEYOND KATTHAMMARSVIK in the east, I stopped to survey the great sweep of Gotland's coastline. A broken shore of white disappeared in the distance, overtaken by the blues of an overarching sky and the ever present Baltic. Leaning against a limestone wall built hundreds of years ago, I noticed that every stone at my feet was a fossil—limestone and fossils being leftovers of Silurian-era reefs that created Gotland more than 400 million years ago.

As I headed back west to Visby, the scimitar wings of swifts cut the sky above fields dotted with six-foot-high stacks of hay. Nearby a tiny nursing lamb pushed violently at its mother's underside. And in the distance I noticed upright stones, clearly hand-carved, that left long shadows across the pasture.

Iron Age picture stones—engravings on loose slabs—have been found all over the island. Some 300 of these memorial stones, unique in Scandinavia, form a record of great value in understanding early people. The earliest stones, from the fifth century, stood at graves, and later ones stood near roadways or open fields where people could admire them.

Many of the stones are now housed in Gotland's Historical Museum, where Malin Lindquist, the curator, has made a careful study of their possible meaning. The largest of all, from the fifth century, stands 11 feet tall and is shaped like an ax head with the cutting edge pointing skyward. The main motif is a spiral whorl or sun and two snakes; below is depicted an oared boat similar in appearance to the ships that transported Egyptian pharaohs. Malin explained the significance of what I was seeing: "The sun and the ship are very early symbols that often go together. The spiral is perhaps the sun rolling across the skies, and the ship is the ship of the dead. The realm of the gods lies at the place where the sun disappears over the western horizon, a place island dwellers know can only be reached by ship. What could be more natural than to sail away to the sunset land of paradise?"

Later eighth-century stones, shaped like mushrooms, are rich in figures, "like ancient cartoons where you can read the story," says Malin. The pictures tell tales of heroes and other epic subjects, such

P art-time brewer Anders Mattson pours golden Gotland dricke *into a waiting keg. This homemade beer, rich and pungent, is brought out for festivals and special occasions. Its strength varies with the taste of the individual brewer.*

as Sigurd the Dragonslayer and Sleipnir, the steed of Odin, depicted with eight legs to show his speed and invincible nature. The mythic horse carries the dead to Valhalla, Odin's home and the last dwelling place for brave warriors.

By the 11th century, dressed stones started carrying runes, the script of Europe's northern peoples with an alphabet of 24 letters. Finally I examined with admiration the last phase of Gotland's famous stones, when carved Christian crosses appeared.

Near Fröjel on the island's west side, in a grassy field overlooking the sea, I came upon a partly restored stone ship grave, an elegant, sweeping form made from huge stones that outline the shape

of a 96-foot-long vessel. Megaliths marked the bow and stern. I assumed that such graves were linked to the Vikings, but in fact they go all the way back to the Bronze Age, at least 1,300 years before the first Vikings ever set sail. Gotland has hundreds of these ship graves. At Rannarve, in a secluded field of ferns and moss, four stone ships lie in a row—a fleet of the dead. The same outsize stone forms the bow of one boat and the stern of the next. On the day I visited, someone had placed delicate yellow flowers there as a remembrance to these long-lost Bronze Age ancestors.

At Vallhagar, I lay in the sunken foundation of a 1,500-year-old house, surrounded by a raised rim of cheerful bluebells and buttercups, dreaming of the owners who had domesticated cats, dogs, cows, chickens, horses, sheep, and goats. They grew cereals, too, and supplemented their diet with wild plants, mushrooms, and berries. At the edge of the field I found troves of strawberries and gorged myself, staining lips and hands with red juice.

Back at the museum, Director Majvor Östergren led me through further historic twists and turns. She started with a subject that invariably grabs everyone's attention—treasure: "Gotland is a living repository of vast treasures, and many are still to be found. Great wealth flowed here from the 9th to the 14th century, most of it in the form of silver coins. More than 145,000 Viking Age coins have been found on Gotland, about two-thirds of all the silver coins discovered in Sweden, and almost every year a major treasure turns up. A year ago, a young couple arrived at the museum door with six-and-a-half pounds of thick bracelets and silver coins, discovered while digging a posthole for a new chicken coop."

To my good fortune a magnificent find came to light while I was on the

A stone ship grave (opposite) lies in a grassy site near Fröjel, overlooking the Baltic Sea. Such Bronze Age monuments date back 2,500 years. Scenes of eighth-century life come alive on the surface of this Bunge Museum picture stone (right). The ship at bottom reveals data about sails and rigging.

island. In the early 1960s a farmer discovered a 1,000-year-old gold bracelet, but he kept it a secret until his death. His siblings found the bracelet hidden in the floor of his home and presented it to the museum on July 17, 1996. Referred to simply as The New Bracelet, it is made of 205 grams (nearly half a pound) of 24-karat gold. Majvor let me hold it; bold and heavy in the hand, the twisted bracelet was still a glowing yellow. She said: "So much treasure exists because so much wealth came here and was hidden in houses, under floorboards, in the walls. It was common to hide silver and jewelry. Luckily, Sweden has perhaps the best protective laws in the world for

archaeological finds, so we can honestly say, 'We have protected the past for the future.'"

Majvor also showed me the museum's Hedgehog Woman, a Stone Age skeleton from 2500 B.C. In the burial site her head was surrounded with hedgehog quills, and around her neck she wore a pouch with five hedgehog jawbones as talismans of protection. The arrangement of bones and remnants spoke to me in a special way, and I felt Hedgehog Woman whispering across the centuries, for I had picked up several hedgehogs on Gotland to look at their wondrous eyes and curious faces, then followed their comical gait in the twilight as they began a night's foraging.

To the far north sits Fårö, an island separated from Gotland by a narrow strait—a world apart that retains much of what is finest in Gotlandic culture. There I visited the farm of Erik and Inga Ohlsson, a couple that cares deeply about conservation.

Inga greeted me at the gate in clogs, a handsome woolen sweater, and long skirt. We fell to talking about her sheep. "Fifty years ago only 70 traditional Gotland sheep existed," she said. "Iron Age skulls and bones of these sheep have been found, so we know they have a long history here." She has a flock of over 60 head, and out back she brought me face to face with a fine example. If ever "wild and woolly" could describe a creature, this was it: A sheep with primeval, wild eyes, curled horns, and fantastically unkempt, thick wool.

The farm's main building is cozy and welcoming, one of its rooms redolent with the smell of sheep and lanolin. Inga showed me the fruit of her husbandry: Fleeces of white, off-white, gray, and dark gray, some smooth, some tightly curled, others long-haired and fluffy, all from her indigenous Gotland sheep. A spinning wheel and loom stood nearby.

Erik appeared, a dignified man at once restrained and eager to talk about the resurgence of preservation and traditional values on Fårö. He proudly led me to his pet project, a field of rye. Only this was no ordinary rye, but an old, neglected type that alone can grow on the carpet of stones that covers the island's isolated north end; it proved so

Lifelong mariner Capt. Bertil Ahlqvist adjusts a ship model inside the headquarters of Visby's Skepparegille, Skippers' Guild, chartered in 1682. The museumlike interior houses centuries of paintings, navigational instruments, models, and documents.

difficult to cultivate that nearly everyone abandoned it. Now Erik and a few others are giving it a chance. "Its quality and taste are better than commercial rye. It creates a home for unique weeds and flowers, so that's important, too, to create a living symbiosis." This seemed a good metaphor for Gotland: people trying to live with the past, holding onto and nurturing things of value.

Erik went on to tell me something about the former way of life on Gotland: "In the past the farmers did many jobs and were fully self-reliant. They grew rye or wheat or barley, kept a cow for milk and cheese and some sheep for mutton and wool. There was time to fish for herring and cod, and to hunt seals

and birds or collect seagull eggs."

On Fårö's windswept north end, where stunted junipers give way to scrub and stone, the surf spray touches everything with salt. Erik, who is a medical doctor, explained to me a little-known fact: "This salt is in a low state of concentration. The Baltic's surface salinity is only 0.7 percent, less than the 0.9 percent in our blood, so we can drink it. But it doesn't taste very good. Sometimes you see the cows and sheep go down to the waves for a drink."

Along the shores of Gotland stand remnant fishing centers of ten or twenty small, weathered wooden buildings, each a perfect rectangle with a sharp, sloping roof. Sometimes an old iron

fire basket still stands as a primitive "lighthouse." Here lie the hulls of long-forgotten dories—small fishing boats for two or three people. "A superstition holds that one never cuts up a boat for firewood or reuses parts of the wood for repairs; we just let the boats 'die' on the beach," said Erik. I saw abandoned boats all over, like broken shells of time and tradition.

On the first Saturday of August, a revitalized tradition grips the people of Fårö. This is the *täckating,* akin to barn raising, a social gathering to rethatch old buildings, bring the community together, and celebrate life. The thatch is not straw but tough sedge, known to locals as *ag* and to science as *Cladium mariscus*. This remarkable plant grows in a wet marsh for seven or eight years before being harvested; there it has time to absorb lime into its cells, making it strong and fire-resistant. Locals told me a well-made ag roof can last 50, 60, or even 70 years.

The roof gathering began soon after dawn with a huge breakfast, provided by university students. Work started slowly, but picked up speed as everyone pitched in. At the edge of the roof, where the ag is most exposed, an experienced thatcher uses a special technique called "twisting the pants" to braid and secure the sedge. Up above burly men use a wooden paddle to "punish the edge" of the ag, to keep it pressed down firmly. No women are allowed on the roof, but on the ground they work as hard as anyone, gathering, collecting, and twisting great braids of sedge. I, too, stayed on the ground to lend a hand, lifting and dragging bundles of the rough stalks. Tradition says the day-long effort must be finished before sundown, and it always is. The placement of fresh, green juniper branches at the roof's two ends brings good luck and keeps away evil.

When the work is finally done, the owner mounts a ladder, carrying a cross encircled by a wreath. This is secured to the center of the roof. An elder of the community bends over and stands on his head, trouser legs blowing in the wind. Beside him a small orchestra, three violinists and an accordionist, plays joyfully. A beer barrel makes the rounds as a final consecration.

Everyone freshened up for the big evening bash, where an age-old menu greets the hungry. Its centerpiece is flounder, here on Fårö a magnificent, plump fish the size of a large man's hand, golden orange on the outside from being smoked. I found it tender and delicious. Food, drink, speeches, and dancing carried on late into the night. I left my newly made friends on Fårö with regret but soon found myself swept up in events that took me back more than 600 years.

In the summer of 1361 Valdemar, the invading king of Denmark, rode through Gotland at the head of his army. He swept aside the farmers' resistance, killing more than 2,000 Gotlanders, and entered the city of Visby through a breach in the southeast wall.

During the early days of August, Gotlanders commemorate this invasion with a flamboyant reenactment, and Visby becomes once again a Hanseatic town. Valdemar's army winds its way to the main square, Stora Torget, where he demands the riches of the city. Three huge barrels are set out, and the king orders the townsfolk to fill them with gold, silver, and jewelry before sundown, as ransom to save lives and protect the city from destruction.

This begins a week of revelry, drama, fun, and portrayals of historic events, known as Medieval Week. The festival gives life to the word "pageantry" with banners of yellow and crimson, blaring trumpets, children dressed as jesters and harlequins in outfits of green and red, a tumbling, ever moving riot of color and sound. Archers and crossbowmen mount the wall at the foot of Powder Tower, overlooking the harbor. Strains of Agnus Dei in plainsong carry across the town.

On the main street of Strandgatan,

*M*edley of treasures at Gotland's Historical Museum proclaims the island's glorious past: glass-bead-and-fluted-metal necklace, silver coins with Arabic script, an ornate, outsize brooch. Finest of all is the solid gold bracelet, a 24-karat Viking Age masterpiece weighing nearly half a pound.

threading Visby's old town, I ran into a 14th-century market come to life. Wool merchants hung up skeins of thick yarn, knitted baby socks, toy animals, and woolen blankets. Bakers shouted out while tossing freshly cooked loaves. A barber snapped together the blades of outrageous clippers, urging one and all to sit for a Hanseatic haircut. The public bath revealed a grinning, lascivious old man in a giant wooden tub, groping at the young washerwoman in a full-length dress who was dousing his head. The smell of grilled sausages filled the air. Metalworkers beat on anvils, milliners lifted their felt and embroidered hats high into the sky on poles, grimy leatherworkers in aprons jostled petite girls selling almonds and sugared rose petals. Wealthy burghers in fine clothes did their best to dodge drunks, beggars, and idiots. A religious procession with choir boys and the strong smell of incense parted the crowd. Sheriffs in armor broke up a street brawl. The fervid acting went beyond the streets and alleys. Even hotel staff and airline hostesses flying to and from Gotland during Medieval Week dressed in 14th-century clothes.

Lars Gustavsson lives on a farm near Grötlingbo and forms part of Gotland's living history. During the fun of

Medieval Week he is known as the flax man. At country markets and gatherings he dresses up in period clothes, dons a coxcomb hat and shows off the entire process of making linen from raw flax. Examples of the green plant with its delicate blue flowers start the display, then come the stiff, gray stalks and the many simple yet ingenious machines that prepare the flax in stages: A dull wooden chopper to break the tough stalks; more refined devices to beat the chips of stalk off the fiber; three sizes of spikes, progressively smaller, through which the flax is combed to make it smooth and shiny. It is finally taken to a special spinning wheel. At the end are displays of fine linen products: place mats, tablecloths, bolts of natural and dyed linen for clothing. "My mother grows the flax, actually, but I think it's important to keep this craft alive—to let others, especially the children, see the old ways," explains Lars.

To SUM UP MY Gotland experience, I paid a visit to Thorsten Andersson, governor of this island county, in his sunny office. He put me at ease right away and began to talk of his years of tenure. "Above all, Gotlanders like and want their independent position. They have a special way of living here—yes, the people are a bit like *Homo insularis*. They take their time to think things over. Where modern man is busy rushing around looking for something, for roots and meaning, here on Gotland we have time to think over our lives and our attitudes, time to reflect. We know who we are. Every year we get 'quality of life' immigrants from mainland Sweden, who feel that on Gotland life's troubles can

Twenty-one-year-old Therese Funk revels in her role as Gotland's Rose Queen, who is crowned each summer in a spectacle of scent and color.

Following pages: Aerial view of Visby reveals a beautifully preserved 13th-century walled city.

be worked out if not entirely forgotten. And part of that good quality of life is the way people really care about the land and the past, about our history and where it has brought us."

On my final day, I wandered down to the seashore, where small clusters of people gather along the waterfront outside Visby's city wall. A kind of happy exhilaration was in the air as friends shared laughter and wine while the sun melted into the sea, leaving behind a magenta halo. Gotland's natural beauty and the strength of its people left me buoyant and optimistic, and I wondered if, as in Viking and medieval times, the island might once again rise to greatness as a cultural meeting place in the center of the Baltic, a bridge between East and West. Thorsten Andersson's parting words rang in my head: "On Gotland the way to the future always seems to lead through the past."

TOMASZ TOMASZEWSKY

A summer bicyclist flying Sweden's yellow-and-blue flag pedals toward one of Visby's northern gateways, St. Göransporten (St. George's Gate) in the city wall. Baltic Sea trade built Gotland into a medieval powerhouse; Visby's massive wall, with more than 40 watchtowers, rose to protect the city's newfound wealth.

Neighbors and friends assist a special roof team at Fårö's annual täckating, *a daylong community ritual of rethatching and fellowship. A well-made roof, created with tough marsh sedge called* ag, *can last more than 50 years. Fiddlers on the roof (right) celebrate work's end with a joyful tune.*

The flower-decorated wreath, hoisted by the barn's owner, marks the success of the day's thatching. A traditional feast of smoked flounder follows, accompanied by drinking and dancing.

otland's sheep, emblematic of the island, provide sheepskins and lustrous wool for sweaters. Paleontologists record bones and skulls of this ancient breed going back more than 2,000 years. Down to a mere 70 head in the 1940s, they thrive once again.

Following pages: Gothic glory of St. Mary's Church commands Visby's skyline. Built of sturdy limestone by 13th-century German merchants, it is the city's last functioning medieval church.

Stark ribs of St. Catherine's Church (left) speak of Gotland's decline after the 14th century. Thirteen great churches, sponsored by local parishes, monasteries, and trading guilds, once flourished inside Visby's city wall. Hard times and population decline caused them to be slowly abandoned.

Such tumbledown ruins have become popular sites for theater and concerts. Musicians of the yearly Gotland Chamber Music Festival (below) warm up before an evening performance within the ruined walls of St. Nicholas's Church.

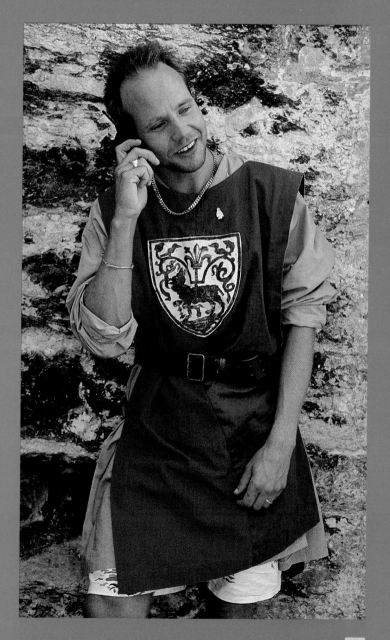

A helmeted knight astride panoplied charger (left) raises his lance in victory to the crowd's cheers. Since 1984, every Gotland summer sees the flowering of Medieval Week, a period of pageantry when bright tent-cities spring up and most residents dress in authentic period costumes from the mid-14th century. High points of the festival are medieval markets and a full-blown tournament. Technology transcends time (right) as an anachronistic mobile telephone allows this medieval merchant on a Visby side street to chat with friends.

*S*crub-in-a-tub (below) proves ever popular with visitors to Gotland's exuberant Medieval Week. For a small fee, pretty girls attend to the washing, and laughter erupts from wooden bathtubs. A gleeful jailer and his prisoner (right) join in a reenactment —part fact, part fable— of Denmark's invasion in 1361; the young virgin, accused of treason, is led through the streets and entombed in a stone watchtower known as the Maiden's Tower.

Following pages: Breath of flame from a fire-eater ignites the night as Medieval Week draws to a close. Street performers and jesters soon disappear—only to return next summer.

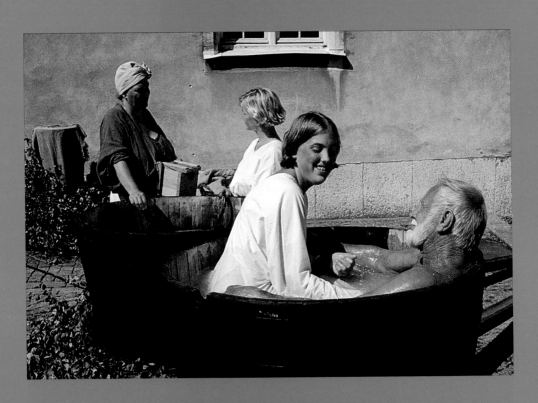

JUAN FERNÁ

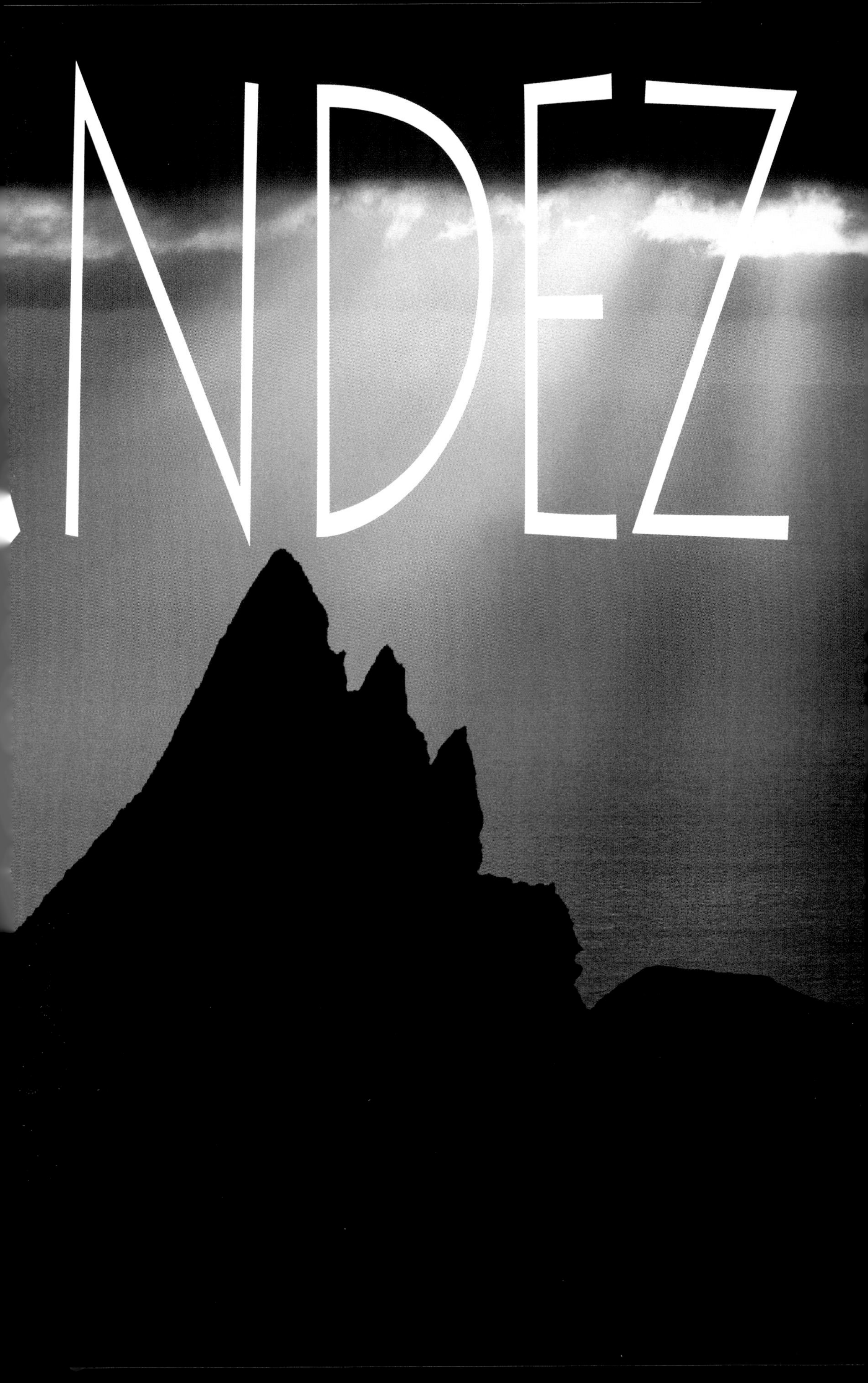
NDEZ

Juan Fernández

By Mel White

Photographs by Miguel Luis Fairbanks

JUAN FERNÁNDEZ ISLANDS

PACIFIC OCEAN

RÓBINSON CRUSOE ISLAND

Cerro Tres Puntas 1,600 ft

San Juan Bautista

Cumberland Bay

To Alejandro Selkirk Island, 102 mi, 164 km

El Yunque 3,002 ft

Villagra Bay

Padre Bay

SANTA CLARA ISLAND

0   4 mi
0   4 km

SOME 400 MILES TOWARD SUNSET FROM CHILE,
THE JUAN FERNÁNDEZ ISLANDS HAVE BEEN A PIRATES'
LAIR, A LONELY COLONIAL OUTPOST, A REFUGE FOR
RARE SPECIES, AND A HOME FOR ROBINSON CRUSOE.
AFTER MORE THAN A CENTURY OF ISOLATION,
RESIDENTS HAVE JOINED THE DIGITAL AGE WITH THEIR
ENDURING COMMUNITY SPIRIT INTACT—SO FAR.

Lush vegetation covers the steep, humid slopes of Róbinson Crusoe Island's high peaks.
Preceding pages: Evening sun silhouettes Cerro Tres Puntas ("three-pointed hill").

itting pretty on a neighbor's mula *(a horse-mule cross), two-year-old Irantzú Aboitis gets a kiss from her babysitter. Four-legged transportation makes good sense in San Juan Bautista, Róbinson Crusoe Island's only town, where unpaved streets link the houses of 500 residents.*

Following pages: Visitors arriving at this dirt airstrip, on Róbinson Crusoe's arid western tip, travel by boat from foam-fringed Padre Bay to the village six miles away.

hree hours west of Chile's sunny Pacific beaches, the pilot of our twin-engine Cessna points dead ahead to a dark shape materializing in the silvery sea mist. It's too bad about the clouds, he says. On a clear day we'd see *una isla de fantasía verdadera*—a true fantasy island.

A knife-edged mountain appears, flanked by jagged ridges and shadowy wooded valleys; soon we're flying along cliffs rising straight up from the wave-battered shore. Curtains of wispy fog flash open on primeval-looking tree ferns, wind-stunted trees, and a dizzying perpendicularity—and then, tantalizingly, they close again. We've arrived, it seems to me, at something as good as a fantasy: *una isla misteriosa*.

Moments later, as suddenly as walking through a door, we're out of the clouds and cruising past what seems to be another island altogether: a barren, earth-tone place, a wrinkled badland. The plane banks around a promontory, and a single thought pops into the heads of all four passengers: *That's* the airstrip?

An English sailor who visited this island in 1709 wrote that "the Land that lies out in a narrow Point to the Westward, appears to be the only level Ground here"—and precious little of it there is. The scar across the moonscape below is well-defined: It begins at one

sea cliff and ends at another. The pilot checks the wind sock and banks sharply; the wheels touch on a downhill slope and we rumble along the red-dirt strip. A dismaying nothingness is fast approaching, but the plane spins neatly in a turnaround just at land's end.

My heartbeat drops back into double digits, and I realize I was wrong about this place. It's definitely *La Isla de Milagros*—Miracle Island.

We transfer our gear to a waiting boat and set off for a village six miles away; the intervening terrain is too rough for any land vehicle to make the trip. Soon we're skirting high black cliffs and pointed spires that pierce the clouds like monstrous teeth. As we round the island's northernmost point, ropy stone intrusions seem to trickle down a massive wall of twisted reddish strata. They testify to a violent volcanic birth, but the boatman has a more poetic explanation: *Lágrimas del viudo,* the widower's tears, he calls them.

All these angular ridges and raw rock make this speck of earth look like something God created when He was only practicing and then hid away so no one would see. Not until the 16th century, that great age of discovery, did it take its place on the sailors' map of the Americas—and thereby hangs no ordinary tale, but one of the most famous adventure stories ever told.

I'm on my way to see where Robinson Crusoe lived.

IN 1704 THE ENGLISH PRIVATEER *Cinque Ports* dropped anchor at one of the islands in the Juan Fernández group, some 400 miles off the coast of Chile. Although the island was small—just 14 miles long by 4 at the widest—it had tall trees, fresh water, and excellent fishing; in the 130 years since its discovery by the Spanish sailor for whom it was named, it had become a supply stop for ships in the area—trading vessels and the pirates who preyed on them.

As the *Cinque Ports* made ready to leave again, the Scottish sailing master, Alexander Selkirk, had a violent argument with the captain, claiming the ship was dangerously unseaworthy. He demanded, perhaps just for show, to be left behind; to his chagrin, he was. As Selkirk stood on shore and pleaded to be taken back aboard, the *Cinque Ports* sailed away—shortly to founder off the coast of Peru with the loss of all lives, save for a handful of men captured and imprisoned by Spaniards.

Four years and four months later, Selkirk was rescued from his solitary existence by Captain Woodes Rogers, commander of another English buccaneering expedition. On Selkirk's return to England he became an early-day media celebrity, thanks to Rogers's popular account of his voyage and a newspaper article by Richard Steele, the famous essayist. In truth, Selkirk was by no means the only sailor to have spent months or years alone on an island, but his story came along at the right moment to capture the public's fancy.

As Rogers related, Selkirk tamed the island's feral cats to stop rats from nibbling his toes at night; at times he sang and danced with his new friends to keep from feeling lonely. He was shot at by Spanish pirates and escaped so narrowly that his pursuers "made water" at the base of the tree in which he'd hidden. When his gunpowder was gone he took to chasing goats on foot and became so fit that he could outrun them even on the most rugged terrain. He made a coat and hat of their hides, sewing with an old nail. When he was rescued, Rogers described him as "a Man cloth'd in Goat-Skins, who look'd wilder than the first Owners of them."

Selkirk's story served as the model for Daniel Defoe's *Robinson Crusoe,* published in 1719. Although Defoe moved Crusoe's island to the Caribbean, and provided him with practically an entire warehouse of supplies to make his life easier, many elements of Selkirk's true adventure remain. Defoe's castaway's tale was an immediate success, and its popularity, as every modern reader knows, has survived nearly three centuries of changing literary tastes. But what of the place that inspired the myth—the real Robinson Crusoe's island?

After the pirates came the sealers, who slaughtered fur seals by the millions, until no more could be found. Mariners discovered another island 110 miles west, and the two took the splendidly literal names Más a Tierra ("closer to land") and Más Afuera ("farther out"). In the late 19th century, a small group of families colonized a village on Más a Tierra, named for St. John the Baptist, and began a tradition of fishing that continues to this day. A few scientists dropped in now and then, discovering plants and birds that existed nowhere else in the world.

The first airplane landed on Más a Tierra in 1966, proving wrong those who said an airstrip could never be built. Around that time, islanders—with the thought of increasing their tiny trickle of tourists—officially changed the name of Más a Tierra to Róbinson Crusoe Island, and of Más Afuera to Alejandro (Alexander) Selkirk. Television arrived in 1986, and the telephone in 1993.

And one more thing: Some time after

landing at the little dirt airstrip not long ago, a writer and a photographer walked up the dock at the village of San Juan Bautista and promptly fell in love with the place.

"Y...M-C-A!" the Village People sing. "Y...M-C-A!" It's 2:30 in the morning at the Disco Brújula, and I'm thinking: If there really are only 500 people on this island, every young person healthy enough to walk must be on the dance floor right now.

In the two days since we arrived, Miguel Fairbanks and I have met a fair share of the population, and some of our new friends are here tonight. Maria, who cheerfully serves us three meals a day at the inn where we're staying, is handing out beers at the bar. Over in the corner is Salvador, the fisherman I met on the dock today, who told me the enormous fish he was carrying, *salmón de roca*, was the best in the island's waters. This is a fine and neighborly spot: Parents sit watching their kids dance, and when the beat slows down a little, they aren't at all shy about getting out there themselves.

The Brújula is not a bad place to contemplate Róbinson Crusoe Island, which exists in ever accelerating transition from an almost otherworldly remoteness to a faxed and digitized modernity. Before air service began in 1966, the island's only connection with mainland Chile—*el continente,* as residents call it—was by a long, tedious, and weather-dependent ocean voyage. Now they boogie to hip dance mixes, their mail goes out every day, and they receive the same instantaneous flood of news the rest of us do.

Local legend claims that Scottish sailor Alexander Selkirk, the real-life inspiration for Robinson Crusoe, found shelter in this cave during part of the four years he spent marooned on the island. A modern entrance framework and a rock wall fancifully re-create the castaway's living arrangements.

It's not the beauty of the island that has charmed Miguel and me so quickly —though it has plenty, from the village snug in the curve of Cumberland Bay to the green slopes of 3,002-foot El Yunque ("the anvil") reaching up like a temple, its top perpetually hidden in the clouds. Neither is it history, though that is ever present, nor an abundance of things to do, for in truth there aren't many. Instead it's this sense of impending-but-not-yet-arrived change, and beyond that the sweet feeling that we're not too late to share a spirit of community already gone from most of the earth. These disco kids are good examples: Though they affect a bit of the hip attitude that their American counterparts have

polished to a high gloss, when you talk with them, they open up as brightly and naturally as an island sunrise.

Among the first things you see as you arrive by boat at San Juan Bautista are two big dish antennas pointed toward satellites somewhere in equatorial space. Just yards away, on the neat little village square, are two metal poles stuck in the dirt of the main street; EMERGENCIA, the sign between them reads, and hanging below are a round metal plate and a beater rod. Bang hard enough and all but the remotest houses on Róbinson Crusoe would hear your cry for help.

IT'S TEN IN THE MORNING, and I'm sitting in front of the Hostería Villa Green, lazy from the breakfast served by our innkeeper, Heidi Green. Apart from being a great cook, Heidi loves to tease and joke with her *yanqui* guests and never comes out second best. From the post office a block away I hear the manual typewriter of Jorge Palomino, the postmaster who doubles as part-time local priest—or is it the other way around? On this late-summer day the temperature is teetering, as it has since we arrived, just between long- and short-sleeve. The villagers say summer hasn't even come this year; Heidi blames it on French nuclear testing.

In much of Latin America, women are reluctant even to say hello to a stranger, but as I sit here, everybody—young and old, male and female—has a smile and a *"Buenos días"* or *"Hola."* Róbinson Green, Heidi's brother, stops to talk, and I tell him how peaceful it seems—it's like a dream.

"Yes," Róbinson agrees, "life is good here. There are no guns, no knives." He puts his hands together, rests his cheek on them, and closes his eyes. "Maybe five deaths a year," he says. "No problems."

I ROUSE MYSELF and walk. The few blocks of streets here are all dirt, but concrete sidewalks go everywhere. This makes perfect sense, since there are perhaps seven cars in town, and long hours pass when dogs sleep completely undisturbed in the middle of the road.

I head uphill, soon leaving the last house behind, and stop at a big wooden sign marking the border of the international biosphere reserve. Apart from being declared a Chilean national park in 1935, the Juan Fernández Islands earned the highest United Nations natural designation in 1977 because of their tremendous number of endemic species. In fact, everything on Róbinson Crusoe beyond the town limits, and all of Alexander Selkirk Island, ranks as a treasure on the same order as the Everglades or Amazonia.

Róbinson Crusoe's ecology is as endangered as it is unique—a too-familiar story on islands everywhere. Just beyond the sign are eucalyptus trees from Australia and Monterey pines from America; if I back up too far to take a photo of the reserve sign, I'll scratch

Reaping the harvest of the sea, lobstermen leave port at daybreak for a long day of tending traps. Fishing brings in 70 percent of Róbinson Crusoe Islanders' income; tourism is a distant second.

myself on bramblebush from Europe, a virulent pest that crowds out native species and climbs higher into the mountains each year. Introduced species have displaced natives in all the island's low places, aided by erosion caused by grazing of sheep, cows, goats, and, most especially, rabbits, which in places teem far beyond plague numbers.

Higher, I begin seeing some of the dozens of endemic plants that have made Róbinson Crusoe famous among botanists: graceful ferns, *luma* and *naranjillo* trees, and *Juan Bueno,* a shrub with beautiful violet flowers. The native woodland is moist, lush, mossy, dark. I notice movement in the branches, and catch a glimpse of a small tufted black bird the locals call *cachudito,* the little horned one; ornithologists call it the Juan Fernández tit-tyrant. Farther on, I spot a much more celebrated local resident. The Juan Fernández firecrown is a gorgeous, brick

red hummingbird with an iridescent forehead that, in the right light, glows like an orange jewel. Islanders call it *el rojo,* the red one; if it or cachudito disappeared from Róbinson Crusoe, they would disappear from the earth.

After climbing 1,700 vertical feet I arrive at a saddle in the ridgeline where, tradition has it, Alexander Selkirk kept watch during his years here. This is, indeed, an excellent lookout, for it commands a panorama of two sides of the roughly triangular island. Tall rock stacks loom above the trail on either side: a frame for an exile's lonely hopes.

To the west the terrain changes from thickly wooded to sere and brown as decisively as if someone had pulled up a green carpet. Lying in the rain shadow of El Yunque, this part of the island seems a different world from the moister eastern half, rolling away in ridges and coves to that singular flat spot where the airstrip lies.

Cerro Tres Puntas ("three-pointed hill") tops the island's backbone like a giant cockscomb. They say on clear days you can see Alexander Selkirk Island above it in the distance, but today I spy nothing but the sheen of the sea and the pale blue of the sky—the same emptiness Selkirk saw day after day, year after year, as he waited for the ship that might rescue him.

FEW OF THE HOUSES on Róbinson Crusoe would be described as more than modest, but yards full of flowers—roses, morning glories, chrysanthemums, sunflowers, cannas, geraniums, and many others—give the whole village an air of perpetual celebration. One day, when Miguel and I stop along a narrow lane to admire an exuberant rainbow of a garden, a woman waves to us from

Fresh from the Pacific, lobster and vidriola (amberjack) pique the curiosity of a fisherman's pets. Most lobsters are sent to the mainland, but many end up in local pots (opposite).

behind a shrub and invites us into her neat frame house—parrot green outside, sky blue inside—for a Coca-Cola.

Clara Araya, we learn, was once married to a grandson of Alfred von Rodt, San Juan Bautista's original chief of colonization. In 1877 he led the effort that finally established a settlement on the island, after failures dating back to the days of Juan Fernández himself. At 48, having had eight children, Clara says she still has a very cheerful personality. "I love to have a good time," she says. "I go to the disco and dance all the dances." Clara is as bubbly as the glasses of soda she hands us, but she frowns a little when we ask her about the changes she's seen on the island.

"We have progress now, with the television and telephone," she says, "but in my opinion life here has lost some of its charm and distinctiveness. We're getting to be like the rest of the world."

On cue, the phone rings. Clara answers, then cups her hand over the mouthpiece. *"¡El barco está llegando!—* The boat is arriving!" Soon we, along with what seems like half the town, are standing at the dock, staring out at a ship rolling in the waves just offshore.

The great majority of the men on Róbinson Crusoe are fishermen—more specifically, lobstermen. While most fish nearby waters, some spend each summer working traps around Alexander Selkirk Island. Today, after many months, these temporary exiles are coming back; Clara's boyfriend is on the boat, and she's one of many anxious to welcome loved ones home.

Before long the dock is swarming with people hugging each other, kissing, laughing, crying. The men are carrying bedrolls, rifles, boxes of lobsters, huge headless fish, slabs of goat ribs. Dogs are coming home, too, and they're barking at the friends they've missed. Live goats on the boat bleat endlessly; men on the dock lasso them by their horns and pull them up. There'll be red meat on dinner tables tonight.

Underlying this happy reunion, though, is a sense of unease. Most years, Clara tells me, the men stay on Selkirk until May; they're returning now, three months early, because the lobster market is no good. Other countries are selling lobsters cheap, and no one can make any profit. People are worried that, when the fishing season ends, they won't have enough money to last through the winter. They're worried, too, that they won't be able to afford to send their kids to high school in Valparaíso, on the mainland, when the fall term starts up.

The next day, Miguel and I meet at the village school with Victorio Bartollo, a witty, rotund, mustachioed man whom everyone respectfully calls Don Victorio. A teacher for 32 years, he is these days instructing children of his former students. About 120 students attend kindergarten through the eighth grade on the island, Don Victorio says. After that, nearly all go to el continente to continue their education. This long-distance schooling exacts a price beyond the financial: Of those who travel to mainland schools, very few return.

"Young people leave and discover a whole new world," Don Victorio says, shaking his head. "Here there is only one television channel; on the continent there are forty. On the continent they discover the use of money; here, you hardly need it. They have a great variety of jobs there. And there's a vast pool of women. We have too many men here— lots of bachelors."

Like Clara, Don Victorio regrets

recent changes on Róbinson Crusoe. "In a sense, the island has lost its innocence," he says. "We're paying the cost of progress. There was more creativity in the days before television. People would meet in the plaza and talk, or play guitars. Where there once was a familial feeling, now people are more solitary. They stay inside glued to the TV.

"We have four sporting clubs on the island, and the kids have begun wearing their colors more—orange, green, red, and blue. They're even buying their street clothes in colors."

"You mean…like gangs?" I ask. "No," Don Victorio says, with a smile. "There are no gangs here. There's no delinquency among the kids. It's a friendly sort of rivalry. It's more the spirit that is injured, rather than the corporeal being of the town."

The island's peaceful soul may be, as Clara and Don Victorio worry, as endangered as el rojo, flitting from bloom to bloom, tenuously surviving in its only earthly home. On the other hand, I think, as we say good-bye to the teacher, maybe the future will be more like that of Juan Fernández's fur seals,

so persecuted two centuries ago. Once thought extinct, they were rediscovered in a small colony on Selkirk in the 1960s; today they've made a strong comeback, and thousands live along the coasts of both islands. Fishermen, who once killed seals because they believed them to be a threat to the lobster catch, now call national park rangers to report animals that are sick or caught in nets.

It's a hope, anyway.

Back at the inn, Heidi asks us if we're going to Villagra tomorrow. This is a valley a half-hour's walk beyond Selkirk's lookout—but in late summer the name means a traditional island fiesta, when free-ranging cattle are rounded up and branded, when people

Remote doesn't necessarily mean out of touch: On weekend nights Róbinson Crusoe's small but lively disco rocks to the beat of the latest dance tunes, from Latin salsa to American hip-hop. The music starts around midnight and may roll nonstop until 6 a.m.

camp out for two nights and barbecue and make merry.

Heidi says she'll pack a lunch for us for the first day, but not to worry about food after that: "People will give you things to eat. Everybody shares—everybody has a good time."

IN A SHELTERED VALLEY overlooking one of the island's prettiest stretches of coastline, tents flutter in a grassy field like red and blue flowers. Kids take turns sliding down a knoll on a piece of cardboard, while below the surf rolls in and the sea foam whooshes out.

"Villagra is an island tradition," Don Victorio has told us, and then, in his melancholy way, added, "but it has

changed." The first thing I notice is two young men playing folk songs on guitar and mandolin. The second thing is a teenage girl playing with her electronic Game Boy machine.

Down the hill a ways men have killed a cow, so Miguel and I wander over and join a gaggle of wide-eyed children watching the butchering. The ground looks as if a small red cloud had rained on this one spot. A man holds up a handful of crimson flesh. "The heart is the richest part," he says, and heads off to his campsite.

Some of the younger men have already rounded up 30 or 40 cattle in a small corral just over the ridge. Determinedly tough-looking in their sombreros and bandannas and sunglasses, they gallop their horses around the crowd, enjoying their cowboy moment. Soon a few men climb into the corral, watching for a chance to make a running leap onto one of the bulls; no one stays mounted for more than a few seconds before being bucked off, to mock cheers of the onlookers.

While Miguel takes pictures, I wander back to where the two musicians, Germán and Julio, have attracted an audience to their impromptu concert. We pass around a bottle of wine, and when that's gone a soft-drink bottle of pisco liquor mixed with something red. The guitar is passed around, too, and when it gets to me I do a couple of verses of "Knock on Wood," which at the moment is as close as I can come to a traditional folk tune. Then I try "Midnight Hour" in Spanish, and I realize I should have quit when I was ahead.

"Is this like Woodstock?" one of the kids asks me.

Toward dusk, Germán takes the guitar and begins sweetly singing a song I haven't heard before, a song they tell me is very old. The joking and laughing stop, and the others softly join in:

"Juan Fernández, eres hija de la tierra,
Prima hermana de la luna y las estrellas—
Juan Fernández, you are the daughter of the earth,
Cousin of the moon and the stars.
You are the mother of the sons you cradle,
You give them a thousand beautiful caresses.
Deep mountain ranges that show
Their imposing peaks in the sea,
Today have become my house and my home.
Come, and believe that God is here."

When the light is right, iridescent feathers vividly affirm the Juan Fernández firecrown's evocative name. Both the hummingbird and the cabbage tree on which it feeds are found nowhere else but the Juan Fernández Islands.

IT'S SUPPERTIME, and a family invites Miguel and me, three college girls from Santiago, and a couple of the cowboys to sit down with them and eat. They give us soup, pasta, chicken, cookies, and tea. They want to know if we have a place to sleep. They ask us if the food is good and how we like it here.

The food is very good, thank you. I like it here a lot.

Later, I walk up the hill and think about leaving this island, think the kind of thoughts that you do at such times, with a full stomach and a cleansed soul and a heart already missing new friends. The Milky Way is blazing above me, and after a moment's puzzlement I realize with a little start that I'm looking at familiar Orion, the Hunter, turned upside down in the Southern Hemisphere. Alexander Selkirk must have watched the slow spinning of these stars countless nights—and, despite his yearning to leave the island, in time he perhaps felt some of the same feelings I have now. After his return to Scotland he built a crude cave-shelter behind his father's house on the Fifeshire coast, where he spent long hours alone, staring out over the Firth of Forth.

No doubt Róbinson Crusoe Island will in time become even more like the rest of the world. Seven cars will become 20, or 50, and San Juan Bautista may put up a stop sign. One television channel will become 100, and folks will spend even fewer evenings talking in the square, and more kids will go off to school and not come back, and they may never learn the words to their island song. But that's someday—not tonight. Tonight, sharing this beautiful landscape with all these good people, it's possible to look out over the campfires to the sea, to look past El Yunque to the moon and the stars, to the hunter turned protector, and believe that the miracles will go on forever.

I n a rough-and-tumble
ballet, soccer players
from two of San Juan
Bautista's sporting
clubs battle in the
annual island
championship series.
The intense but friendly
rivalry between clubs
is a lively aspect of
social life on
Róbinson Crusoe.

*S*wimmers (below) gather at the local "beach," a concrete boat ramp. Like other islands in the archipelago, Róbinson Crusoe was built by ancient volcanoes; its rocky coastline offers little easy access to the sea. Typical is the scene (opposite) at Villagra Bay, where residents look down on rugged cliffs and wave-battered ledges.

Following pages: San Juan Bautista crowds along a narrow strip of flat land bordering Cumberland Bay, its waterfront dominated by the gymnasium (at right), the municipal wharf, and satellite dishes for television—one channel—and telephones.

Bright smiles light the faces of children on their first day back in school after summer vacation. Students attend classes from kindergarten through eighth grade on the island, after which most travel to el continente—*mainland Chile*—to continue their education.

igh spirits rule during the annual rodeo at Villagra Bay, where Germán Recabarren plays for an appreciative audience. After free-roaming cattle are rounded up, a calf (below) is marked with the owner's brand.

Following pages: A Villagra camper chops wood for an evening bonfire, celebrating an island tradition that has lasted for 80 years.

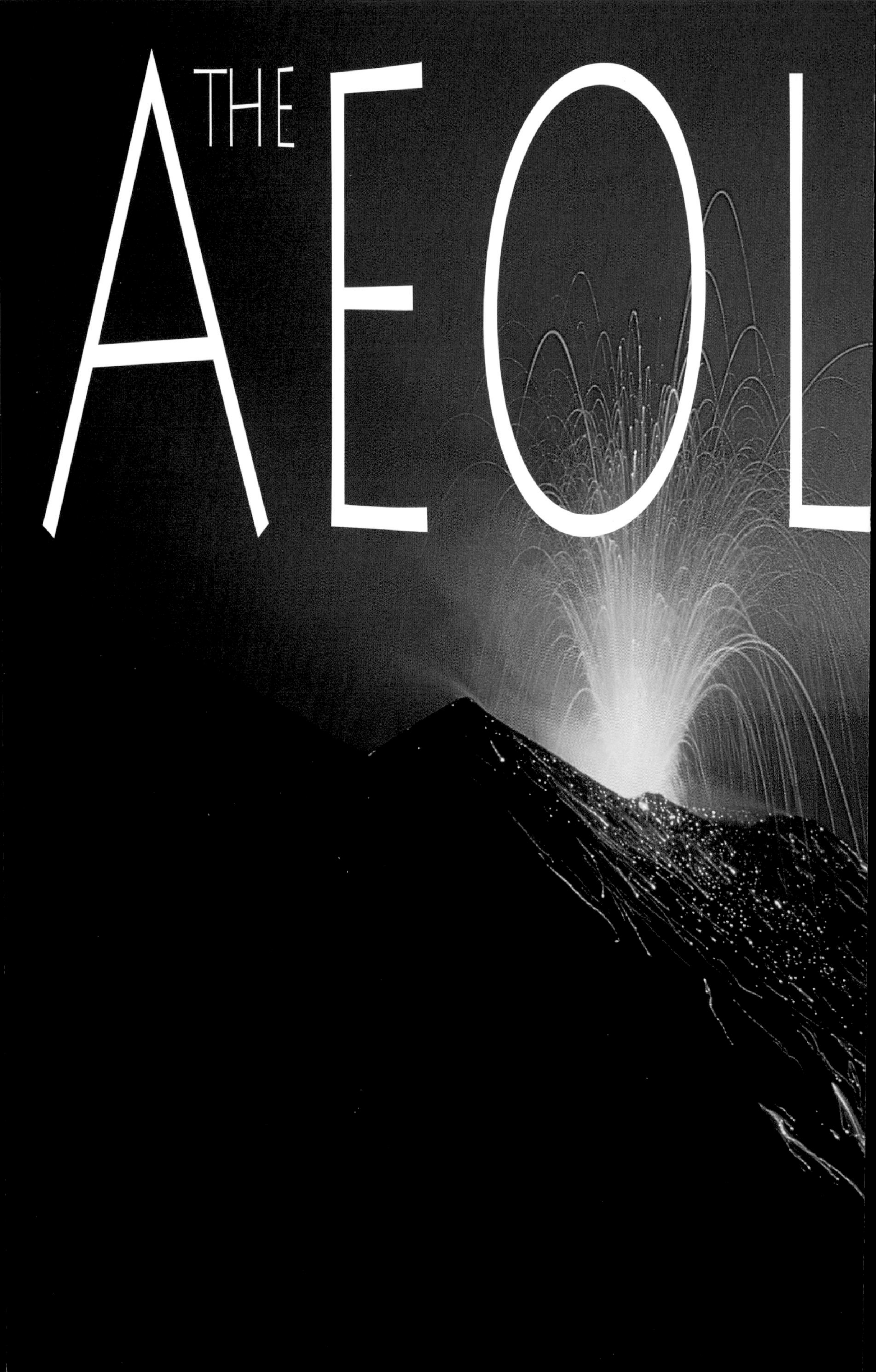
THE
AEOL

The Aeolians

By Leslie Allen

Photographs by Jay Dickman

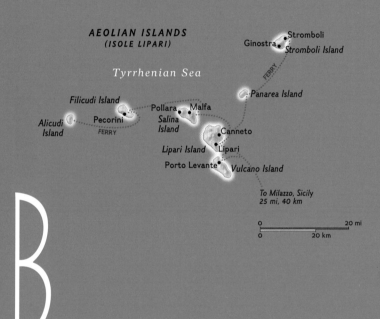

**AEOLIAN ISLANDS
(ISOLE LIPARI)**

Tyrrhenian Sea

Stromboli
Ginostra · Stromboli Island

FERRY

Filicudi Island
Panarea Island

Pollara · Malfa
Alicudi · Pecorini · Salina
Island · Island
FERRY

Canneto

Lipari Island · Lipari

Porto Levante · Vulcano Island

To Milazzo, Sicily
25 mi, 40 km

0   20 mi
0   20 km

ORN OF FIRE AND BURNISHED IN MYTH,
ITALY'S AEOLIANS HAVE NURTURED HUMAN CULTURE
FOR ALMOST 6,000 YEARS. HOMER WROTE THAT AEOLUS,
MASTER OF WINDS, RULED THE SEVEN ISLANDS.
TODAY, ELEMENTAL RUGGEDNESS, INCLUDING TWO
ACTIVE VOLCANOES, HELPS PRESERVE A TIMELESS AURA
DESPITE PROXIMITY TO THE MAINLAND.

Sunset silhouettes a fishing boat and Filicudi's 302-foot La Canna—"the cane."
Preceding pages: Molten lava fountains from a volcanic vent on Stromboli.

*C*hildren frolic along the waterfront seawall of Alicudi, most westerly of the Aeolians. On all but Lipari, education ends after the primary level; older students face grueling off-island commutes.

Following pages: Cosmopolitan by comparison, Lipari boasts more people than the other Aeolians combined. Banner-bright fishing skiffs tie up at Marina Corta, a cozy hub of Lipari town.

The hydrofoil rose on its metal sea legs, kicked the glassy Tyrrhenian into shards, and sped northward. Off the stern, sea foam veiled Sicily's ragged coastline. Ahead, I squinted toward Vulcano and Lipari, the southernmost islands of Italy's Aeolian archipelago, less than 20 miles away. But nothing broke the horizon, which melted into a blur; and for nearly an hour, only the droning engines quieted the sense I had of traveling in a timeless, placeless limbo. Finally, Vulcano appeared, looking untethered as a cloud that wafted between the sea and the brilliant sky.

In the region's uncanny light, visitors often first glimpse the seven volcanic islands as apparitions. There's good precedent for that illusion. Writing some 2,800 years ago, Homer sent war-weary Odysseus to a "floating island"— probably Lipari—ringed by a smooth wall of cliffs. There Aeolus, lord of all the winds, comforted the wanderer with "numberless dishes," and the music of flutes. But things ended badly after Odysseus' men opened a sack of wind, and Aeolus banished them. And to this day, Aeolus remains a fickle presence in these islands, raising choppy seas that isolate the Aeolians for days on end in winter—or suddenly, mysteriously becalming sailboats.

The Aeolians have long been a place of many gods. The ancients revered the fire god, whom the Greeks called Hephaestus and the Romans Vulcan. During my two weeks in the islands, I constantly admired his handiwork, which gives the Aeolians their streaked lava cliffs, their white pumice slopes, and their jumbles of dormant, grassy craters; under the active, seething craters of Stromboli and Vulcano, admiration gave way to awe and even fear.

The sea god Poseidon, it was said, applied finishing touches to Hephaestus' creation, ringing the islands with spiraling sea stacks and cool grottoes. Ashore, the ancient cult of Dionysus lives on in silky Malvasia wines from Salina, in all kinds of homemade liqueurs (I particularly liked a shockingly potent lemon concoction offered by an elderly woman dressed in black), and in the sense of theater that enlivens every conversation.

LIPARI, VULCANO, SALINA, Stromboli, Panarea, Filicudi, and Alicudi: This little cluster has many contradictions. For millennia, people have in turn found the Aeolians welcoming and hostile, beautiful and barren, poor and bountiful. "The Aeolian kitchen is very simple," insisted chef Lucio Bernardi, carrying on a multigenerational tradition at Filippino, a restaurant in Lipari. "There are only a few dishes." Then he proceeded to bring forth so many elegant seafood plates and airy desserts that I was reminded of Aeolus' "numberless dishes."

In the mid-1800s, all of the islands— hundreds of families—counted just 24 boats for transportation and fishing. Now, fleet hydrofoils, the Aeolian workhorses, link the islands to each other, and to mainland ports; hulking ferries bear cargo, while ships bring in most of the islands' supply of fresh water. But as I was to discover, the Aeolians still feel remote—a place apart, lost in time in many different senses.

Like most visitors, I first stepped ashore on Lipari, the archipelago's largest island (14 square miles) and by far its most populous, with some 9,000 people. Since a majority of these residents crowd into Lipari's namesake town, its twisting alleys and pastel buildings boast as many people as the rest of the Aeolians put together. Things change dramatically at the town limits, though. A ride into the hilly interior took me back centuries, past abandoned farmsteads and tiny churches.

A sheer-walled fastness of rhyolitic lava dominates the town of Lipari. Its soaring flanks jut aggressively into the water, plowing between minuscule harbors. After the Tunisian pirate Ariadeno Barbarossa sacked Lipari and enslaved its people in 1544, Spanish occupiers reinforced the Greek and Norman defenses with massive bastions. Now simply Il Castello—"the castle"— to the Liparesi, this natural citadel, crowned with religious buildings and old defenses, is the historical epicenter of life in the Aeolian Islands.

By the 1940s, however, when archaeologists Luigi Bernabo Brea and Madeleine Cavalier first started working there, 20th-century Lipari was a long-forgotten backwater. "There was absolutely nothing," Brea told me, motioning through his office window in the Castello. "The buildings were a Fascist prison from 1926 to war's end, then a camp for displaced persons, and then they were deserted."

No one, not even the archaeologists, had the vaguest inkling about the treasures lying beneath their feet. "I knew nothing about these islands'

importance beyond a few hints in the Greek legends," said Brea.

As it turned out, just a few yards from where we sat chatting, Professor Brea and Dr. Cavalier started uncovering a past far older, richer, and better preserved than anyone could have imagined. As Brea explained, "Preservation is due to a very strange geological phenomenon around here. The mistral and the west wind—the prevailing winds here in the Aeolians— sweep over the plateau above us, blowing very light volcanic ash onto the Castello and the town below, and increasing the ground level very rapidly. Here on the summit these ash deposits are ten meters high."

Ten meters—about 30 feet: A cross-section of 6,000 years of Aeolian life, civilization upon civilization, so gently preserved that potsherds from this acropolis are used to date finds from other Mediterranean sites. Grassy terraces stepping away from each other represent mind-boggling leaps of time; but on each level, tight mazes of truncated walls bring to mind the persistent sense of danger felt by the countless generations who crowded atop this natural fortress.

A SUBSTANCE THAT GIVES Lipari's stony beaches their shimmering dark glint sparked the seemingly endless quest for domination of this island. As Brea explained: "For a tiny island, Lipari had enormous importance in prehistory because of its obsidian. There were very few other sources of this black volcanic glass, and Lipari's was the best quality." Before the discovery of metal smelting, obsidian was the sharpest material

SISSE BRIMBERG

known, and Lipari's obsidian blades were coveted from France to Dalmatia. "For 2,000 years, the obsidian culture prospered," he said. "By about 3000 B.C., the settlement of Lipari had more people than any other in the western Mediterranean." No later culture would survive nearly as long. New peoples drove older ones out at closer intervals: Sicilians, Greeks, Etruscans, Carthaginians, Romans, Byzantines, Arabs, and Normans, among others.

To walk through the Castello's Regional Aeolian Archaeological Museum, one of Europe's best

collections from antiquity, is to see, in objects of everyday life, the rising and ebbing of cultures over a vast amount of time. "What we have," Brea said, "are testimonials to the different activities of different periods. It's not a collection of beautiful things."

Maybe not, but the collection includes objects of awesome beauty. Thousands emerged from the brief golden age that blossomed when Lipari was a thriving outpost of Magna Graecia—Greater Greece—between 476 and 251 B.C. Satyrs and maenads frolic across one krater, or wine jar, from this period. On another, my favorite, a naked female acrobat springs into a handstand before Dionysus while her companions gape in mock amazement. Then there are the small things once lovingly placed in the tombs of young children: A little statuette of a mother bathing her baby in a small basin; delicate vases shaped like animals; a doll with movable arms.

The Liparesi of the classical period were great lovers of theater. They left behind a large, varied collection of masks and statuettes—more than 1,200—depicting characters from the favorites plays of their time by Sophocles, Euripedes, Aristophanes. Menander, master dramatist of Athens's New Comedy, is represented by hundreds of pieces: Squinty-eyed brothel keepers, smooth-browed courtesans, straining slaves, pot-bellied bumpkins.

AND THEN THE LAUGHTER STOPPED: The Roman fleet wreaked merciless revenge on the Aeolians for their allegiance to Carthage during the Punic Wars. Tiny, but strategically located, the islands continued to be buffeted by the winds of empire right into the modern era. Warfare repeatedly emptied them, said historian Giuseppe Iacolino. "Starting from nothing, the islands were repopulated at least three or four times."

All the while, natural phenomena—volcanic eruptions and powerful earthquakes—were keeping pace with man-made cataclysms. Their frequency results from the fact that 17 major composite volcanoes, which form the islands and numerous seamounts, crowd along several active fault lines in the Mediterranean area's youngest and most restless basin.

Still, these titanic natural forces, with their awesome powers of destruction, have their benign side. Just south of Lipari, the hot springs of Vulcano drew imperial Romans by the legion to take the waters, though the island was considered too dangerous for prolonged stays. Since then, the volcano has become increasingly active. The last major explosion ended in 1890, but more recently there have been releases of liquid sulphur—the abundant substance that gives parts of Vulcano a smell that seems made up of strong cheese, salt water, and spent fireworks—or, if you prefer, rotten eggs.

These days, though, Vulcano's few residents and its many visitors seem impervious both to the odor and to the looming presence of an unpredictable and increasingly menacing volcano as they head for the Acqua del Bagno—"bathing water"—hot springs. The natural pool is set in a crumbly grayish moonscape streaked with rust and ocher, and pocked with cone-shaped fumaroles. There, bathers wallow in the warm, fizzing mud. Faces smeared with the whitish stuff bob surreally above the murk. Impassioned testimonials assert the springs' power to cure everything from arthritis to run-of-the-mill malaise.

It was hard to shake the eeriness of the whole scene, as people went calmly about their leisure in a realm where creation and destruction collided. This assault on the senses called for an antidote. I found it when I went for a hike across the low isthmus that connects the main part of Vulcano with a much tamer trio of small volcanoes forming its northern knob, Vulcanello. Half a mile from the mud baths, the sulphurous fumes and colors gave way to the sweet smell of yellow broom and the spiciness of oleander. Instead of the sound of fumaroles belching, I heard a dog bark in a distant yard. Wind rustled through eucalyptus woods. I felt as if I

had walked through an unseen gate, back into a recognizable place and time.

Stromboli's volcanic contrasts are even more startling. Northeasternmost of the Aeolians, the island *is* its volcano—or, more precisely, the third of it that breaks the surface of the Tyrrhenian and climbs another 3,000 feet to its summit. Clusters of little white houses, stacked cube upon cube like a child's block construction, cut right angles against seaside jumbles of lava and bands of black sand. The northside Sciara del Fuoco—the boulder-strewn "highway of fire" that rolls from crater to sea—is one of the blackest, bleakest, most lifeless places on earth. But to the east, volcanic soils yield lemons larger than grapefruits, acres of red geranium shrubs, and walls ostentatiously wrapped in purple bougainvillea.

Stromboli is literally as different as day and night. The Sicilian sun, flashing off the sea and the hot cloak of a live volcano, bleaches the dark island into an overexposed image; by day, the crater is an occasional distant rumble, a puff of smoke, or, if you glimpse its activity from a boat, an unseen giant juggling boulders into the sky. But by night, eyes turn to the fire high in the darkness, and Stromboli is again the Lighthouse of the Tyrrhenian, a mariners' beacon for uncounted centuries.

Night is the time to experience the volcano up close, to make a twilight pilgrimage to Hephaestus' nimbus.

ipari fisherman Enzo Tomarchio (opposite) casts his nets for a varied catch. The Aeolians' scorpionfish (right), one cookbook avows, is unmatched for its sweetness.

Because the three-hour, 3,000-foot climb to Stromboli's summit and the descent in darkness are somewhat perilous, not to mention arduous, most hikers choose to make the trip with a guide. Mine, a compact, bearded Strombolean named Mario Zaia, had rippling muscles and a limber, even gait to show for 20 years' and two thousand trips' worth of climbs.

Falls, fatigue, and dehydration claim occasional minor casualties, but the hazards of the climb have little to do with Stromboli's constant eruptions—most of the time. The crater itself, more than 600 feet below the summit overlook, endlessly reswallows the fiery explosions of magma and gas that it jets hundreds of feet into the air every few minutes. Every few years, lava rolls down the Sciara del Fuoco and into the sea in a burst of steam. Even rarer are the cataclysmic paroxysms capable of dropping ten-ton bombs of lava on the village below.

But just a week before I climbed the volcano, a single abnormal spasm had showered the summit with molten cinders. "It happened at midnight," said Mario, slicing thirst-quenching lemons during a break in the climb. "Most of the people had left, but there were 15 campers huddled in one spot, and molten rocks fell just a meter away. Imagine if one of them had stopped to tie a shoe."

"Destiny" was Mario's explanation for the absence of injuries—or worse—during these rare events. It became my mantra as, breathing hard, I forced my feet to follow Mario's on slopes so steep that sometimes his feet were at my eye level. "Destiny," I exhaled, and then, before I could see the crater, heard a roar so intense that I could only think of it as something that came from

within me, like a thunderclap to the solar plexus.

The sun had set and we had just reached the summit plateau when the orange molten fountains and the red-hot boulders came jetting up to eye level from the crater. *"Piccola cosa,"* scoffed Mario, "a small thing." A few minutes later, it happened again, and then again. *"Piccola cosa,"* I thought, was Mario's mantra. But then the explosions became bigger and louder, and Mario just stared. "The only thing that's always the same about Stromboli is that every night it's different," he said later.

One characteristic of all volcanoes called strombolean, after this one, is that they erupt more or less constantly. Still, no matter how eagerly I awaited the next explosion as I watched from Stromboli's summit, each one, when it came, was unexpected. Caught off guard, time after time, by the flash and jolt, I had to swallow an impulse to get up and run away fast. Then I would look forward breathlessly to the next eruption.

Attracting and repelling, Stromboli, the volcano, is a magnet that has helped galvanize an island that almost died. Motioning to other visitors and guides at the summit, and then toward the crater, Mario said, "This volcano is like the factory that keeps this island going." For visitors, a night atop the volcano—or a boat ride to the base of the Sciara del Fuoco—offers thrills of a lifetime. For islanders living under the volcano, Stromboli has meant something else altogether.

Retired schoolteacher Mariannina Renda Russo witnessed the paroxysm of 1930 and its aftermath of falling rocks, hot avalanches, tsunami, wildfires, and acid rain through the eyes of a seven-year-old child. The horror of the eruption was mixed with more puzzling aspects, too. "I remember people passing by with chairs over their heads to protect them from the cinders," Mariannina said. "I remember thinking how strange that was."

Long after the ash cleared from the air, the effects of the eruption lingered on in Stromboli: "After 1930, so many people were afraid to go on living here. My father was the island's doctor, and he worked hard to calm them. But people were beginning to hear about Australia and America, and they used their fear of the volcano as a reason to go."

Brilliant white walls faded. Rounded outdoor bread ovens grew cold, and rush trays for drying grapes and figs no longer adorned the loggias of slim-columned courtyards. Then, in 1950, help arrived from an unlikely quarter: Swedish film star Ingrid Bergman and Italian director Roberto Rossellini. "Everyone knows Bergman was beautiful," said Mariannina whose family gave her a place to stay on Stromboli. "But she was also very kind."

Bergman's and Rossellini's passion, as endlessly reported to gossip-craving audiences worldwide, stirred as much interest in the island as did Rossellini's grim portrayal of Stromboli in the film of the same name. "Bergman's admirers were the first tourists," said Mariannina, who, with her husband, Domenico, built the island's first hotel, La Sirenetta.

While summer now swells Stromboli's population, the number of year-round residents on the island has continued to fall. Almost all 400 of them live in the island's larger village, usually called just Stromboli, on the northeast coast, but 25 hardy inhabitants call westside Ginostra, the island's only other village, home.

In *Stromboli*'s climax, Ingrid Bergman desperately makes her way from the larger village to Ginostra by climbing the volcano to cross the island on an ancient footpath. There is only one other way to reach the tiny hamlet: Via a harbor cleft in the lava boulders that, with careful maneuvering, can accommodate two small boats. Larger vessels, such as hydrofoils, stop several hundred yards offshore, relying on tenders to transfer people and goods ashore.

ON THE DAY I VISITED, Ginostra's only motorboat was out of service for a paint job, so the substitute tender was a rowboat. It was also the day when a supply ship arrived for its twice-weekly call at Ginostra. While the *Giovanni Bellini* rocked in the swell, the tender's oarsman, rowing gondolier-style, made numerous trips between ship and harbor. Gas canisters for the town's restaurant...wooden crates of tomatoes from Palermo for a store...cardboard boxes of Central American bananas... dozens of other cartons...water pipes... sundry packages...all were duly loaded and unloaded.

"Life wasn't meant to be easy," laughed Giovanni Merlino, donkey in

tow, making his fourth trip up the zigzagging concrete path that links the pint-size port with the village hundreds of feet above it. The proprietor of one of Ginostra's two stores, he was in the process of restocking, a task that demands a beast of burden in a town without cars or trucks. As the animal stomped at flies, its cargo of crates shifted precariously.

Dressed in a navy blue polo shirt, Giovanni Merlino didn't break a sweat, though it was at least 90°F under the noonday sun. Clearly the Ginostra native preferred this season to others. "Winter is uncomfortable," he said. "We only have solar electricity, so in winter we depend on gas lamps. With rough seas, we can sometimes be isolated for two weeks. Then the Italian Navy has to send in helicopters with supplies."

Up and down, back and forth. Meanwhile, Uli Stulgies, tanned and wiry, and *his* donkey were making the same trek, transporting cement from pier to town to higher slopes beyond. Originally a professional actor in Munich, Uli arrived in Ginostra 15 years ago. Finding work in a place like Ginostra is never easy, but Uli has managed. "I'm a company," he told me; "I have two donkeys." In addition to being Ginostra's all-round maintenance man, he is a volcano guide and the leader of the environmentalist faction.

Environmentalist faction? I noticed that as they crossed paths leading their donkeys, Uli and Giovanni didn't have much to say to each other. Even in a town of 25 residents, politics speak loudly. Giovanni and Uli, it seemed, disagreed about what kind of, and how much, new development and construction would be most appropriate for Ginostra—the size and location of a new pier, for example, and whether or not the town needed a new road that, for the first time, would allow people to drive.

Uli and Giovanni did seem to agree about one thing, though: Despite its immense charm, Ginostra needed some kind of help to save it from extinction. "Poor people can't do what I do," said Giovanni, "which is to send my wife and children to Lipari during the winter." Uli noted how hardship, especially winter's isolation, had caused many residents to leave: "There is a lack of living traditions in Ginostra. You can find pieces of worked obsidian from Neolithic times, but you can't find old people."

LIKE GINOSTRA, the smaller Aeolians are places where time has visibly stopped more than once. Panarea, near Stromboli, and the westernmost islands of Filicudi and Alicudi are each not just one place but several as a result.

On a day so bright and hazy that sky and sea merged and boats seemed to float in a void, I sailed around Panarea, the littlest Aeolian, and its uninhabited archipelago of volcanic outcroppings. Beneath the soaring spires of one offshore islet, Basiluzzo, I snorkeled in search of an ancient dock built for a Roman village atop the islet. Why did the Romans come to this bit of rock? To punish their political prisoners? To guard a seaway? No one knows.

On the island's southern tip a finger of sheer-walled basalt curls around a small bay of gem-like clarity. On this promontory, Punta Milazzese, a Bronze Age people flourished about 34 centuries ago. Walking amid the remains of their oval stone huts, you can't help but wonder if they appreciated the matchless beauty of this slender cape. Archaeologists only know that they

chose it as a natural fortress in a time of great danger. Nevertheless, newcomers from the Italian mainland conquered them and destroyed their village and their culture.

These days on Panarea, affluent newcomers from Milan and Turin have spruced up the little blue-trimmed houses deserted by 20th-century islanders; an imported dolce vita blossoms every summer.

If the Aeolian people have gone, the story of their hardscrabble existence remains in the narrow, rock-walled terraces that cover Panarea and the other islands. On Filicudi, these abandoned terraces climb near-vertical pinnacles. On Alicudi, which is a single volcanic cone, they rise, along with the village, some 2,000 feet from sea to summit. The difficulty of farming these sunbaked slopes without a reliable supply of fresh water was one of the main causes of widespread emigration at the end of the 19th century and after the two world wars. Overpopulation caused the fragmentation of land into ever smaller plots. Overfishing was a problem too, and there was no industry to take up the slack. Those who had left helped keep things going by sending money home.

Unlike the other islands, Salina has freshwater springs, and is the most verdant Aeolian. But when a plague of phylloxera ravaged Salina's fabled grapevines about 1890, time stopped on that island, too.

"It's really unbelievable how Aeolians move around so much," said Clara Rametta, as we lunched on the shady terrace of her small hotel in Malfa, a village on Salina's north coast. In fluent English, she described her own family's

Only the trattoria's lights burn at Pecorini a Mare, where Filicudi's ribbon of roadway runs out. Wanderers and artists find silence in the hamlet, which was drained by postwar emigration. Abandoned farming terraces attest to the island's dwindling population.

odyssey, starting in Salina. "My grandmother was born in Buenos Aires, then moved to Malfa; she went to the United States after she married. My mother was born in Melrose, Massachusetts. There were so many Aeolians there that they used to have an annual fundraiser for a scholarship for a student. My mother returned, and I was born here."

Clara herself went to college in Boston and earned her master's degree in psychology. After she married her husband, Michele, who was working in Malfa's town hall, she commuted four

hours by hydrofoil three times a week to work as a psychologist in the Sicilian city of Messina. "It was crazy. I wanted to live and work on Salina, so we decided to build a hotel." Malfa had only one.

Rising from its placid harbor in a maze of low stucco walls, Malfa appears unchanged from the artist's rendition on the cover of the sheet music for "Salina," published in Massachusetts in 1941. The composer, F.A. Russo, dedicated the song to "my boyhood memories of the Eolian Islands, and my affection for the Eolian people." Clara had also stumbled upon the sheet music for another wartime Russo song, "Marching to Berlin and to Tokyo." Its cover showed a World

War I photograph of the composer, in U.S. Army uniform, alongside a 1942 photograph of his smiling son, Dante, as a Marine Air Corpsman. Clara told me that Dante was later killed in combat.

Michele, now the Signum Hotel's chef, and Clara had served what Clara apologetically called a "simple" lunch: fresh mozzarella, tomatoes, olives, capers, bread, white wine, and little almond pastries. Except for the Sicilian cheese, everything came from Salina itself. And the palette on my plate—its freshness, and the care with which all the ingredients had been chosen and arranged—somehow reflected the thoughtful revival of Salina itself that seemed to be under way, as abandoned

farms are reclaimed for vineyards, and the island's delicious capers enjoy renewed interest based on their reputed cholesterol-lowering powers.

Salina's capers are only one of more than 70 local plant species that have medicinal value, according to Dr. Sergio Giani, a pharmacist and expert on botanical medicines. After he published a book on the Aeolian Islands' medicinal plants, some Salina residents organized to turn one of their island's richest areas into a nature reserve in 1981. Today, Monte Fossa della Felci—"the crater of ferns"—the Aeolians' highest summit and one of the two volcanoes that form Salina, is a park that preserves altogether some 500 plant species.

As we climbed the volcano's slopes, Sergio pointed out dozens of flowers, leaves, and stalks, describing traditional uses confirmed by modern science. "Salina's flora is the richest of the Aeolians," he explained. "The soils are so varied, and the millennial presence of man has contributed to the enormous variety of species." Here and there amid the glades of pine and chestnut and the open slopes were startling signs of that human presence: An ancient refuge carved out of a lava overhang; domed stone huts built four centuries ago to watch for pirate ships; and at the fog-shrouded summit, bits of obsidian, pottery sherds, and the remains of huts of a sacred site used from Neolithic to Byzantine times.

Sergio's passion for saving the endangered knowledge of folk medicine sounded a resonant chord. Just a few days earlier, I had walked to the summit of another island, Alicudi, with another passionate spirit, a retired customs agent from Padua named Antonio Fulgione. Past the empty homes, past the solar panels of a few urban refuges, past the abandoned church, past the forgotten grottoes as cold as natural refrigerators, the seemingly endless stone staircase finally led to an ancient, moldering compound: home, wine press, kitchen, Alicudi's oldest stores. Antonio was restoring them inch by inch so that visitors might have a sense of a past era of self-sufficient living.

Lost in time: For people like Sergio and Antonio, intensely squaring off against the loss of traditions and

Boaters probe Filicudi's Grotta del Bue Marino, once the haunt of its namesake monk seals.

Following pages: Valdichiesa— "valley of the church"—parts volcanic peaks that define Salina; Monte dei Porri rises from its twin's shadow.

knowledge, time was of the essence. Others were reaching back farther, and finding, in the more distant past, an enduring source of artistic inspiration. On Filicudi, Marina Clemente was creating whimsical, evocative sculptures from found objects. Mythology was her muse. "These islands were mythological places for all the Mediterranean people long before Odysseus came here," she said. "For me that is always present in the images I create."

And back on Lipari, where I had begun my Aeolian travels, I met sculptor Giovanni Spada. He had devoted six years of his life to copying in perfect detail the ancient statuettes, deities, and theater masks in the museum. Now, he held a few for me. As this handful of gods stared up, their faces, frozen in clay, spoke across millennia of the Aeolians themselves: islands both lost and found in the immensity of human time there.

V ulcano's main crater, dormant since 1890, becomes an otherworldly playground (left) for a visitor. Cappuccino-colored mud pools (below) have been highly regarded since Roman times for their therapeutic value.

*P*rovisions proceed
by donkey toward
Ginostra, on Stromboli.
The port, a teardrop of
an inlet, holds only two
tiny craft. Tenders ferry
people and supplies
from larger vessels
offshore. On Salina
(below), children head
home from Malfa's
village shops.

Pennants of crimson peppers frame a Lipari storefront and the proprietor's mother, while strings of garlic and potted basil complete the Italian tricolore. *Despite unreliable rainfall, volcanic soils bring forth luxuriant local produce in sunny kitchen gardens. Barter once played its part in* the islands, although the use of coins dates back to the third century B.C. The cash economy makes inroads on a Stromboli byway (below), where the chance meeting of fisherman and housewife seals a sale.

"Orchid of the Aeolians," the caper flower (left) belies its delicate appearance, carpeting cliffsides in lavender and cream through spring and summer. Nipped in the bud, the plants yield handfuls of cucuncios for pickling. While the berries figure widely in local cuisine, the caper's medicinal uses found note as far back as Ecclesiastes. Fruits of the vine, especially the Aeolians' white Malvasia grape, have earned favor with wine fanciers worldwide. In his Filicudi vineyards (right), Stefano Zagami inspects the ripening harvest with a friend.

ascading bougainvillea softens Stromboli's cubelike dwellings. Offshore, a lighthouse rides the choppy summit of sheer-walled Strombolicchio— "little Stromboli"—a petrified neck of the Aeolians' oldest crater.

Following pages: Beyond Lipari and its seafront town of Canneto rises Vulcano with its smoking volcano.

ABOVE AND FOLLOWING PAGES: SISSE BRIMBERG

Hewn from the
summit of a sunken
crater, fishermen's
storage sheds rise above
the tide line at Pollara,
on Salina. On Lipari
(below), vulcanism
yields the economic
legacy of still-active
pumice mines.

Following pages:
Ragged spires of
Spinazzola shadow
a boater's paradise
off Panarea.

INDEX

R. IAN LLOYD

Sunrise gilds mangroves and driftwood in the Andamans.

NOTES ON CONTRIBUTORS

LESLIE ALLEN, a former staff writer, lives in Washington, D.C. She has contributed to many Special Publications and other Society books, including chapters on archaeology and anthropology. In addition, she now freelances for the *New York Times* and other publications.

IRA BLOCK, a New Yorker, has been a freelance photographer for NATIONAL GEOGRAPHIC and TRAVELER magazines since the mid-1970s. He has also contributed photographs to three Special Publications and to archaeological books.

PATRICK R. BOOZ, is a freelance writer living in Sweden. He grew up in Asia and writes frequently on Asian subjects. His interest in history and geography stood him in good stead in this book and in the recently published Special Publication *Great Journeys of the World*.

JAY DICKMAN, a freelance photographer, lives in Colorado. Winner of the Pulitzer Prize for feature photography in 1983, he has contributed to articles in NATIONAL GEOGRAPHIC magazine and to several Special Publications, the latest being *Our Inviting Eastern Parklands*.

MIGUEL LUIS FAIRBANKS won the World Press Photo Award for feature photography in 1990. A freelance photojournalist, he makes his home in California. Fluency in Spanish aided him in this chapter assignment and in article assignments for NATIONAL GEOGRAPHIC in the 1990s.

R. IAN LLOYD, born in Canada, has been based in Singapore since 1980. He has contributed the photography to more than 30 books on Asia. His freelance work for the National Geographic Society has included photography for TRAVELER.

MEL WHITE, a freelance writer living in Arkansas, specializes in travel and natural history. His writes frequently for TRAVELER and has contributed to several books, including the Special Publication *Our Inviting Eastern Parklands*.

SIMON WINCHESTER's lifelong fascination with islands led him on a 50,000-mile odyssey around the British Empire in the 1980s, resulting in his book *The Sun Never Sets*. He lives in New York, and is hard at work on a marine series.

JOSEPH R. YOGERST, a freelance travel writer and editor, is based in California. His travel books include *Vietnam: Land of Nine Dragons*, which won the 1992 Lowell Thomas Award. His work also appears in many other publications.

ADDITIONAL READING

The reader may wish to consult the *National Geographic Index* for related articles and books. The following sources may also be of interest: **Andamans**—S.T. Das, *The Andaman & Nicobar Islands: A Study of Habitat, Economy, & Society;* L. P. Mathur, *History of the Andaman and Nicobar Islands;* Jayanta Sakar, *The Jarawa;* N Iqbal Singh, *The Andaman Story;* V. Suryanarayan and V. Sudarsen, editors, *Andaman and Nicobar Islands: Challenges of Development.* **Pitcairn & Norfolk**—Herbert Ford, *The MISCELLANY of Pitcairn's Island;* Government of the Islands of Pitcairn, Henderson, Ducie, and Oeno, *A Guide to Pitcairn;* Merval Hoare, *Norfolk Island;* Jane Wesley, *Quality Row, Kingston, Norfolk Island.* **Gotland**—Mary Alderton, *Sweden;* Gotland Tourist Association, *Gotland and the Hanseatic Town of Visby: A Guide for Visitors;* Roger Öhrman, *Gotlands Fornsal: The Historical Museum of Gotland;* Arthur Spencer, *Gotland.* **Juan Fernández**—Wayne Bernhardson, *Chile and Easter Island;* Daniel Defoe, *Robinson Crusoe;* R. Megroz, *The Real Robinson Crusoe;* Tony Perrottet, editor, *Insight Guides: Chile.* **Aeolians**—P. Manetti and J. Keller, editors, *The Island of Stromboli: Volcanic History and Magmatic Evolution;* Philip Ward, *The Aeolian Islands.*

ACKNOWLEDGMENTS

The Book Division wishes to thank the many individuals, groups, and organizations mentioned or quoted in this publication for their help and guidance. In addition, we are grateful to the following: B. S. Banerjee and staff, Directorate of Information, Publicity, and Tourism, Andaman and Nicobar Islands; Richard K. Barz, Australian National University; Joergen Birman and Camilla Bozzoli, NGS Translations Department; Alice Buffett, Norfolk; Jim Dorman and Chris Murray, Lord Howe Island Museum; Herbert Ford, Pitcairn Islands Study Center; Les Garraway, Norfolk Island Visitors Information Center; Paul J. Lareau; Vishvajit Pandya, Victoria University of Wellington, New Zealand; Howard L. Phelps; Luciano Siracusa and staff, Aeolian Tourism Office; Victor Springer, Smithsonian Institution; Åsa Wikström and Elisabeth Eriksson, Gotland Tourist Association.

Library of Congress CIP data
Islands lost in time.
    p.   cm.
    Includes bibliographical references and index.
    ISBN 0-7922-4231-9 (deluxe). —ISBN 0-7922-3651-3 (reg.)
    1. Islands. I. National Geographic Society (U.S.). Book Division.
G500.I87 1997
910'.914'2—dc21
                                        96-54853
                                        CIP

Composition for this book by the National Geographic Society Book Division. Printed and bound by R. R. Donnelley & Sons, Willard, OH. Color separations by American Color, Glen Rock, NJ; CMI Color Graphix, Inc., Huntingdon Valley, PA; Digital Color Image, Pennsauken, NJ; Nashville Electronic Color, Nashville, TN; Phototype Color Graphics, Pennsauken, NJ. Dust jacket printed by Miken Companies, Inc., Cheektowaga, NY.

Visit the Society's Web site at **http://www.nationalgeographic.com**.